Jeremy Sideris

Thinking Originally and Writing Well

A Practical Guide to Composition from the Frontlines

ISBN: 1-4392-4410-3
ISBN-13: 9781439244104

To order additional copies, please contact us.
BookSurge
www.booksurge.com
1-866-308-6235
orders@booksurge.com

DEDICATION

For my beloved Writing Center staff, with whom all is possible.

Introduction

Rhetoric In The University Classroom

The subject of this book is rhetoric. Defined most generally, rhetoric is the act or art of persuasion. A rhetor, then, is simply a person who attempts to persuade another person to think, to feel, or to do as the rhetor so wishes. However, an old saying, "If wishes were horses, beggars would ride," comes to mind. It is not sufficient for the rhetor to merely persuade another person to understand his or her point of view; rather, a rhetor may be considered effective only if his or her call to action is indeed acted upon. In this way, one can imagine the public arena as the site of many competing rhetors and rhetorical messages. This is especially true with regard to the university classroom.

My definition of rhetoric appears to be based on the overt manipulation of one person by another, but rhetoric is not necessarily a cynical endeavor. Human communication in the West, after all, tends to be centered on the establishment of individual point of view and the search for group consensus. Nevertheless, rhetoric can be "multiple," and more than a few titles of books on the subject contain the word, "rhetorics." Given this book's subject, I start our journey together by describing the three competing rhetorics found generally in the classroom.

As one who teaches rhetoric and composition, I am aware of dozens of competing messages within a given classroom, but these can be placed conveniently into a few larger rhetorical frameworks I describe as: the classroom itself, the professor, and the students. Although the classroom, the location where most of our teaching and learning takes place, is central to our shared goals, it has ironically received the least scholarly attention. Many professors ask themselves,

"Where am I teaching this semester?", but one wonders if this question is centered more on faculty convenience and travel time and less on the arguments the classroom spaces are making. Further, a professor might like to assume the students' attention is solely on him or her during class; however, humans are visual animals. Students will take their learning environment in while the professor speaks, but what exactly is the classroom saying? During class, a professor may expound on the students' limitless future possibilities while the classroom suggests something very much different. My own classrooms are the color of old mozzarella. Though the rooms offer ample sunshine, the sunlight works unfortunately toward presenting the walls' dinginess. Newer classrooms I have taught in were painted an almost antiseptic white; not a wholly bad thing in itself, but I was nevertheless reminded, in the absence of visual warmth it was I, the professor, who must provide the "color" for my students. Research regarding the psychology of color suggests light shades of blue, green, and yellow will put students at ease, while enhancing their creativity. One wonders if walls made gray with age argue the opposite.

The reader might assume the points I have just addressed are better left to department heads and administration, those who are more likely to fill out requisition forms, but we ought to remember our daily experiences with our classrooms make us excellent witnesses to the classrooms' possibly negative rhetoric. One last question in regard to arguments made by our classrooms, is added technology the students' friend or foe, bears mention. Just as row-upon-row of tall computer screens may make it difficult for serious students to see the front of the classroom, the screens provide convenient places to hide for the more work-averse students. In short, dreary paint may deaden the students' senses and a jungle of technology argues for the quite unnecessary separation of professor from students. In a way, a professor must be "bigger" than a classroom's technology.

The rhetoric surrounding professors is very much nuanced. A professor naturally believes in the inherent worth of his or her subject, but the professor should not feel much consternation if students at first do not extend the professor's subject the same weight. A professor ought to "sell the steak and the sizzle." One's genuine excitement in a subject will promote interest among students in the subject. On the other hand, the promotion of rote or mechanical learning may argue to the students the subject is one to be gotten through, boring even to the professor. Further, the less a professor speaks directly to his or her students, and the more a professor relies on technology (i.e. Powerpoint), the less the professor's worth is suggested. To this end, I once overheard a student speaking of another professor say, "he'd save me a lot of time if he would just email his presentation." Further still, a professor should not underestimate the rhetorical nature of dress and personal style. Dressing formally will appeal to students who crave an authority figure, but wearing a business suit may put off the more informal students. The opposite is true as well. Students will perceive a mousey individual as a mouse and a stylish individual as having flair.

Beyond the rhetorical messages put forth by the classroom and the professor are the rhetorics offered, consciously and unconsciously, by a course's students. Given their sheer numbers, students may be thought of as having the most diverse set of rhetorics; different values and expectations will be expressed by students of different skill sets, from the advanced student writer to the beginning writer to the functionally illiterate student. A multiplicity of student backgrounds, too, will come to the fore. It is not unusual to find students of vastly differing economic, ethnic, gender-related, political, regional, religious, and sub-cultural points of view sitting within ten feet of one another, interacting, and challenging the validity of each other's rhetorical message. Indeed, the university classroom is perhaps second only to the typical Department of Motor Vehicle office in its ability to provide the casual observer a swatch of humanity and lived experience. Not all students will embrace difference; some students will interpret the rhetorical positions of others as personal affronts, and will vocalize their anxiety or will more passively choose a desk farther away from opposing rhetors. Other students will embrace difference, and will call upon their peers to voice their rhetorical positions during class discussion. Drafting a classroom's cultural and ideological maps are fairly simple tasks after a semester's first two weeks.

Every paper assigned to university students is based on rhetoric; that is to say, each paper is an exercise in persuading another person, the reader, to think, to feel, or to do as the author so wishes. Writing papers is evidence of art imitating life: Students entering a classroom enter a rhetoric-charged environment; students writing papers capture that environment's energy.

Who Is Your English Professor?

Many students today mistakenly assume the gaining of an ability to write well is similar to the buying of a super-sized value meal at the local fast food drive-through. All they need to do is pull up, pay, sit quietly until something substantial is handed to them (be it burgers and fries or, in the case of writing classes, passing grades), and once the sale is completed, leave quickly. Although few of these students would purchase a super-sized value meal as a remedy for life-long poor nutrition, many students will come to class believing a short term investment in one or two writing courses will somehow cure years of piecemeal reading and writing practice.

Quite a few students view the knowledge gained from a writing course as a simple commodity and as a quick fix to long-nurtured problems with English. Your English professor does not share these common assumptions. On the contrary, your professor's many years of schooling have taught him or her that a 100-level writing course is the mere first step to learning how to write well. Further, your professor will tend to view education more as an abstract concept that develops over an indeterminate period of time rather than as any concrete or tangible product. Knowing how your English professor's various identities (scholar, person, citizen, even actor) shape his or her beliefs then becomes of critical, primary importance to your success as a beginning writer.

The title, "English professor" can be a bit misleading. Although some literature scholars do teach 100-level writing, the course does not concern itself much with literary theory or its applications. "English 101" is not, for example, "Introduction to Modern British Literature." On the other hand, the writing course is not centered wholly on grammar, either. Most colleges and universities have upper-level courses dedicated specifically to grammar. Instead, your writing class gives itself to a study of rhetoric, defined earlier as the act or art of public persuasion. Higher education today tends to view rhetoric, especially its written form, as perhaps one of the most important paths to cognitive development because it encourages students to think originally and write well. Most colleges and universities tend to nevertheless call their rhetoric courses "English" for the sake of continuity; departments of rhetoric were largely absorbed into English programs during the early twentieth century. Thus, it can come as some surprise to students that many English professors today actually hold advanced degrees in rhetoric and its analysis and not in English per se. Perhaps "writing professor" is a better title.

Your writing professor likely considers him or herself a rhetorician, one who eagerly studies the interesting ways people harness the unique power of words when attempting to persuade others. Rhetoricians are known also for assigning their students many types of literature to read, not as a general exercise in literature appreciation, but instead as a series of autopsies whereby students are asked to dissect each text's argument, or specific attempt at persuasion. Grammar is addressed by writing professors similarly, insofar they believe their students must know how not to blunt an argument's impact with poor sentence structure. Beginning writers may expect to work a great deal during their comparatively short time with their rhetorician; five or six papers of varying lengths form a writing class' average semester workload.

A writing professor is a scientist. When a writing professor guides you through careful dissection of an assigned text, and you begin to notice the very strict attention to detail with which your writing professor takes apart the author's work, you, too, will share in the immense joy of discovering the text's rhetorical strategy, its systematic, persuasive maneuvering. It is here your writing professor wants you to start seeing yourself as such a scientist. He or she will certainly expect you to experiment with rhetorical strategies the class has discovered, perhaps by modifying and employing the text's more successful tactics in your own drafts while abandoning those tactics considered weak. Still, a text is not exactly a pickled frog lying belly-up on a cold aluminum examination tray. Your writing professor knows full well the power of a text's words lives long after the work has been made available for public consumption.

A writing professor is an artist as well. Like paint on a canvas, the power of words is found in their deliberate arrangement. Words are the colors on a writing professor's palette, sentences are the brushstrokes, and paragraphs form the color scheme. Your professor, an author him or herself, takes delight in the art of writing, and when away from his or her own drafts, is quite an avid reader. It is not unusual for your writing professor to enter class excitedly with excerpts taken from a newly discovered reading he or she considers a masterwork. Then again, your writing professor will also bring to class examples of poor writing—bad art—so as to mark ineffective rhetoric's distance from effective rhetoric. Your active participation in this shared criticism is essential. Your writing professor knows for you to be an artist like him or her, you have to be committed fully to your art and the extended discussion of it.

A professorship is one of the few positions in the United States today that offers open encouragement to think creatively upon but one subject in a fairly job-secure environment. Writing professors, for instance, are paid to think at-length about rhetoric and its composition almost exclusively. They are promoted when they teach the subject well to their students and add to existing theory publicly through the writing of books, journal articles, and conference papers. Thus, your writing professor's life is a busy one, but more importantly, it is a life probably much less chaotic than your own.

Put simply, full-time students registered for five classes are made to divide their attention five ways, especially if most of their classes are electives. Homework divides the students' attention further. During the school week, students with full-time, 15-credit hour course loads may expect about 45 hours of homework if each of their professors assign just higher education's minimum of three hours of reading; the students' time spent with school work will almost double when writing papers. If other real concerns, such as the ever-rising costs of tuition and maintaining a home and vehicle force students to work full-time, 40-hour a week jobs, students will soon find themselves with, again at minimum, 85-hour work weeks.

Given the tremendous workload encountered by freshmen, it is somewhat understandable they would choose to be passive or submissive students. Students for whom time always appears short will desire convenience most. In their otherwise sincere efforts to dedicate enough time to all of their classes, students will make routine memorization of a course's most basic information a greater priority than finding any meaningfully practical application of the information. They will further prefer lecture-based courses over discussion-based courses. Lectures give students the convenient summaries they crave, while discussions compel them to take time to wrestle with the subject under discussion until they come up with their own understandings of the material. Like the students who see themselves as too busy to engage and apply course material actively, students for whom comfort is the greatest priority will neither want more than the most basic information needed to pass, nor will they push themselves to become energetic, vocal members of the class. For these apathetic students, "just getting by" is often enough and they will tend to bring little more to the classroom than themselves. Standing in the way of convenience-minded and apathetic students is the university or college, which has historically demanded active or assertive learning.

Admittedly, convenience is considered an important virtue in the marketplace. The general American public has been long exposed to persuasive marketing campaigns. These campaigns have led many people to believe they, as educated consumers, are full members of a global economy, and are thus worthy of being served at a moment's notice. Belonging to the general public, a number of first-year students will arrive at school viewing convenience as their natural expectation. After all, the marketplace's rhetoric convincingly describes convenience as a necessary part of basic customer service and not as a scheme for increasing sales. Nevertheless, your writing professor will define efficiency differently.

A dynamic teaching method begins with the setting of a few open-ended goals. The 100-level writing course sets two chief objectives for its students: competency in college-level reading and writing. Combined, these two objectives form a breathtaking task; one your writing professor is not always sure will be accomplished fully in the short time offered by the one or two semesters most students are required to give to the study of rhetoric. Your writing professor's learned skepticism is based on his or her understanding of success. Years of teaching experience have shown your writing professor that academic success does not follow a uniformly straight progression; rather, the path to academic success is convoluted. No two people will enter a 100-level writing course with exactly the same set of skills and deficiencies. A writing class with 25 students may find success and failure expressing themselves in 25 different ways.

One student, for example, joins a writing class unable to put a sentence together. The student achieved some success when he became able to create a fully developed paragraph. However, this limited degree of success was lessened when the student remained unable to craft a whole essay by semester's end. Another student joins a class already able to write a complete, high school-level paper. She, too, achieved some success when her writing began to demonstrate college-level thought. Even so, this important step forward was lessened as well when the student's move from high school to college-level thought was not made complete by semester's end. In each case, these classmates have worked hard and have achieved a measure of individual success, but both will also need to dedicate yet more time to learning how to write at college level. Classroom dynamism, then, is defined as the students' level of continued energy given to improving written work. Students who work attentively against limitations, while developing strengths are believed to be working in a dynamic manner.

Your writing professor will view a healthy sense of competition among students as an important indication of classroom dynamism. Active competition suggests to a writing professor his or her students are taking pride in their work, holding their progress to strict account, and remaining wholly unsatisfied with the status quo. Your writing professor, however, does not want you to express this competition with the sharing of grades. Knowing what grades your classmates have received on their papers will do you little good. If you learn your classmates have scored lower than you, you may become dangerously overconfident in your own writing ability, and you may not work as hard in the future. Similarly, if you learn your classmates have scored higher than you, you may lose what confidence you have in your writing ability, and you may become frightened unnecessarily. Rather, your writing professor wants you to express this sense of competition through lively class participation. Nothing discourages your writing professor more than a silent, cow-eyed seat filler.

Students tend to learn quite a lot from their classmates. By listening to your well-reasoned arguments, your classmates will become more well-reasoned speakers themselves. Such lively class participation offers the further benefit of helping your classmates to become better writers. Students who have learned to speak thoughtfully in class will soon write in a more thoughtful manner when at their computers. On the other hand, a quiet writing class is not indicative of a healthy sharing of arguments and counterarguments. Nor does a passive group of students suggest much of a competitive learning environment. To show pride, not vanity, in your learning is to demand thorough clarification of new ideas openly and often. Indeed, the ideal response to statements made in the writing classroom begins with: "Yes, but—". Calling for the opinions of others and listening actively to what others have to say allows you to discover for yourself what you do not know. A competitive student, then, desires learning most.

Writing professors are extraordinarily outgoing people. Their work demands they be so, but it is the writing professors' natural sense of curiosity that has led them to pursue their trade in the first place. Studying how language affects life, how words and their corresponding images are used to define and manipulate reality, writing professors engage society and its many forms of communication often. It is not unusual, for example, to find your writing professor at many of the places you visit. You will likely see your writing professor at bookstores, clubs, coffeehouses, concerts, diners, fairs, libraries, malls, movies, music stores, political rallies, student activity centers, theatres, and video stores for the simple reason these places are where many of society's ideas are introduced, expressed, and discussed today. In other words, your writing professor does not view popular culture or general society negatively because rhetoric takes place squarely in these most public arenas. Moving about in society, your writing professor cannot afford to be shy. Your writing professor likewise does not consider shyness among students a virtue.

True, a number of students will join class believing remaining quiet or speaking softly is a clear sign of respect for one's professor. However, your writing professor understands there is quite a difference between adding your interesting ideas to the subject under class discussion and whispering to the classmate sitting next to you of the six-pack your roommate had funneled the night before. Your writing professor wants to hear from you often; he or she wants you to make a name for yourself. You then need to ask yourself, "would anybody in class know I am gone if I were to stop attending?" Yes, most students realize there is a time to listen, but they should also know there is a time to act. Genuinely shy students will be encouraged strongly by their writing professors to enroll immediately in a voice and movement class offered by their university's Theatre Department as this course goes far in removing the students' crippling stage fright. Coy or falsely shy students, on the other hand, will nevertheless be asked to contribute fully to the class discussion. Hiding behind an open book or looking away or into space is of little use because such avoidant, sheepish behavior draws your writing professor's attention to you quickly.

Whether you realize it or not, you bring much to say with you to class. At heart, your writing professor sees him or herself as similar to you. Everyday, you and your writing professor take an active part in the increasingly complex, often uncertain, twenty-first century American life. Though your writing professor will have likely read more than you, and will have certainly written more than you, he or she is sure your life experiences are equal to, and in some important ways, more interesting than his or hers. A writing professor has only to consider the many viewpoints students bring to university to know students' lives are rich. Any given writing class will, for example, consist of students of widely varying ages. These students will further come from diverse economic, ethnic, political, regional, religious and social backgrounds. Students from different national backgrounds will be present, too, as will be those who hold various sexual orientations and gender identifications. Adding to the writing class' diversity will be students with differing physical abilities. Together, your class will reveal the depth found in lived experience. Your writing professor will call upon you to discuss how rhetoric shapes the perspectives students express in class.

Lively class discussion promotes basic rhetorical analysis, a systematic examination of ideas and strategies important to the art of public persuasion. On the other hand, the reading you perform outside of the writing classroom, whether as part of your homework or done for your own pleasure, lets you move well beyond rhetorical analysis. Reading encourages even more thoughtful application of rhetoric. For one, students who read daily are typically the first in a writing class to recognize the importance of rhetorical synthesis, the combining of several ideas revealed by rhetorical analysis in order to form an original understanding of the topic at hand. Books have opened many doors to new ideas and continue to do so today. Next, well-read students are also among the first able to triangulate or unite three distinct sources of information basic to any 100-level writing class: the arguments put forth by an assigned reading, the thoughts of your writing professor and classmates, and your own opinions. A class discussion that fails to refer to outside sources can easily become a conceit or self-important bull session. Reading allows the student to view rhetoric's existence outside of the writing classroom, off campus, and in the larger world of public ideas.

Rhetoric is employed aggressively in all manner of published and online texts; therefore, your choice of what to read is almost less important than your decision to read every day without fail. Persuasive messages abound in American society today, and rhetoric is an important part of our cultural landscape. Even politicians and members of the news media who claim to "cut through the rhetoric" knowingly use this familiar phrase in an attempt to persuade others to believe they are presenting information more honestly than others. Examples of persuasion are so common in America that study of rhetoric does not have to start with the most traditional source of information, the book. Indeed, different reading materials and approaches to reading are seldom contradictory to one another. For instance, an analysis of fashion magazine content and feminist commentary describing the construction of social identity will provide equal encouragement to students researching how gender is defined and policed in twenty-first century America.

Your frequent reading of a variety of texts demonstrates to your writing professor your activity of mind. When you show a vocal interest in a subject brought up in class, your writing professor is pleased with your participation. However, when you move this interest beyond what was said during class discussion, and actively seek more opinions through reading, your writing professor is impressed by your commitment to learning. Nevertheless, the very idea of reading frightens a number of today's students mightily, and many students are reluctant to even try. It is not that most students enter the writing class unable to read. Rather, the great fear of reading some students carry with them is the result of a lack of practice with the printed word. Compare the act of reading to jogging. The more you run, the easier it becomes for you to jog longer distances, and you will soon forget the physical pain brought on by your awkward first attempt on the track. The same is true with reading. Training yourself through daily reading allows you to read and understand more in less time, and your initial embarrassment will be replaced with confidence. It is that simple.

Most reading-based difficulties under-prepared students face can be attributed to vocabulary acquisition. A statement heard commonly in many writing classrooms, that "College-level reading is so confusing!", speaks volumes to your writing professor. This honest comment suggests a student has run into unfamiliar, perhaps intimidating vocabulary. To this, your writing professor will offer the student a practical suggestion based directly on learned experience: keep next to you a general purpose dictionary while you read general literature and a scholarly or specialized dictionary when you read literature written by members of a specific field of study. So doing, the student may indeed find him or herself using a dictionary to define what seems to be every other word, but that is okay. Like the beginning runner who, slowly ascending a tall hill for first time, almost needs to remind him or herself to put one leg in front of the other, the under-prepared student will be adding to his or her knowledge one word at a time. Such dedication over the course of a semester will certainly not place the under-prepared student on an equal footing with a student who has read actively since early childhood, but doing so will nevertheless set a thoughtful student on the path to continued learning.

Your writing professor will help maintain your levelheaded optimism with open encouragement and advice while you tackle your college-level reading assignments. He or she has taken the class, too, and empathizes with your struggle. However, you create your own luck. Your choice to succeed or fail in any class is your own to make. A student's grades are earned; a student's grades are not assigned. Just as writing professors will not take credit for a student's success (it is, after all, the student who has put forth the great effort), a writing professor will not accept blame for a student's failure. It is the student who has chosen not to dedicate him or herself to the work at hand. Thus, a student needs to address difficulties with reading and writing immediately if he or she hopes to master college-level writing. Remember, your writing professor wants you to succeed. A writing professor's hardest task is to watch a student allow him or herself to fail.

Explanation Of Grades

A grade is a number of points signifying the value of a student's work. Students entering Freshman Composition are often unaware of how writing professors judge papers, but rest assured, your writing professor judges each student's paper according to a grading rubric. A grading rubric summarizes a paper's goals and offers an explanation of each kind of grade. The differences between one grade and another grade rest on how closely a student's paper meets criteria established in your writing professor's rubric.

It is important to remember what exactly a grade is. A grade is a writing professor's judgment of a paper's quality; a grade is not a writing professor's judgment of the student who has written the paper. Too many students convince themselves their writing professor holds a personal grudge against them after papers are handed back. Again, your writing professor has written a grade on your paper, and not on your forehead.

Below is a grading rubric typical of many writing professors. You are encouraged to use it as a basic checklist prior to handing your papers in.

The paper of very fine quality
(A-/ A)

Thesis Statement: Simple to find, believable, unique, refined, perceptive, and understandable.

Rhetoric: All points made build upon one another and flow without interruption. The argument is clear, logical, persuasive, and strong. Ideas are fresh and stimulating. Author addresses and nullifies counterarguments. The reader is made to think about the paper's subject matter in new ways because the author makes original connections to researched materials.

Back-up: Author provides an example for every idea brought up. Each example relates to its paragraph's topic sentence. Author introduces and explains all quotes, and all quoted materials are cited correctly.

Arrangement: Apparent, logical, and appropriate for the kind of paper assigned. Transition words and phrases abound. All paragraphs have topic sentences and most have transition sentences.

Syntax: Grammar is almost flawless, and word choice is brilliant. No spelling errors are found. Author employs punctuation and citation style correctly.

The paper of fine quality
(B+ / B)

Thesis Statement: Shows potential, but is perhaps a bit imprecise, or lacking in perception or uniqueness.

Rhetoric: All points made build upon one another. The argument is clear, logical, and persuasive. Ideas are neither wholly fresh, nor stimulating. Author recognizes counterarguments, but does not nullify all of them. The reader is made at times to think about the paper's subject matter in new ways because the author makes original connections to researched materials now and again.

Back-up: Author provides examples for most ideas brought up. Most examples relate to their paragraphs' topic sentences. Author introduces and explains all quotes, and all quoted materials have been cited correctly.

Arrangement: Apparent and appropriate for the kind of paper assigned. Missing transition words and phrases cause the paper's flow to jerk. Most paragraphs have topic sentences, but a few transition sentences are absent.

Syntax: Grammar contains an occasional mistake, and word choice appears well thought out. Some spelling errors are found. Author employs punctuation and citation style correctly.

The paper of average quality
(C-/ C+)

Thesis Statement: Is perhaps blurred, unperceptive or unoriginal. Suggests a limp argument may follow.

Rhetoric: Not all points made build upon one another. The argument is unclear often, logic may not always be evident, and the argument is not completely persuasive. Ideas are seldom fresh or stimulating. Author does not mention counterarguments. The reader is not made to think about the paper's subject matter in new ways because the author does not make original connections to researched materials.

Back-up: Author provides examples for some ideas brought up. Some examples relate to their paragraphs' topic sentences. Author does not introduce and explain all quotes, and only a few quoted materials have been cited correctly.

Arrangement: Neither apparent, nor wholly appropriate for the kind of paper assigned. Frequently missing transition words and phrases almost eliminate the paper's flow. Few paragraphs have topic sentences, and most transition sentences are absent.

Syntax: Grammar is problematic, and word choice centers often on clichés. Spelling errors are found frequently. Author employs punctuation and citation style incorrectly.

The paper in danger of failing
(C / C-)

Thesis Statement: Hard to find or simplistic, and is almost wholly unoriginal. Tells reader a limp argument will follow.

Rhetoric: Few points made build upon one another. The argument is naïve or unclear, logic is seldom evident, and the argument is hardly persuasive. Ideas are neither fresh, nor stimulating. Author does not mention counterarguments. The reader is not made to think about the paper's subject matter in new ways because the author does not make original connections to researched materials.

Back-up: Author provides few examples for ideas brought up. Not many examples relate to their paragraphs' topic sentences. Author throws in quotes haphazardly. Quotes are introduced and explained only rarely, and almost no quoted materials have been cited correctly.

Arrangement: Neither apparent, nor wholly appropriate for the kind of paper assigned. Frequently missing transition words and phrases eliminate the paper's flow. Few paragraphs have topic sentences, and most transition sentences are absent.

Syntax: Grammar is notably problematic, and word choice centers almost wholly on clichés. Spelling errors are found frequently. Author employs punctuation and citation style incorrectly.

The failing paper
(D+ / D / D- / F)

Work suggests neither understanding of the assignment, nor much effort paid to the assignment. Paper is a headache for the writing professor due to the paper's essential problems with thesis statement, rhetoric, back-up, arrangement, and analysis.

In the end, a good research paper consists of an original, interesting argument, an array of respected research materials that will defend your point of view, and free-flowing grammar. On the other hand, a poor research paper consists of a common, boring, infantile argument, a lack of respected research materials to defend your point of view, and jerking grammar. Put even more simply, your writing professor wants to look forward to the pleasure of reading your papers. On average, each writing professor grades about 500 student papers a semester. Your paper will only stand out from the crowd if your paper gets your writing professor to think in a new way, if your research shows you know what you are talking about, and if your use of grammar is not tedious. After you have made a name for yourself, your writing professor will likely read your paper first because it is the kind of student writing he or she looks forward to most.

A Brief Note Regarding How To Talk To Your Writing Professor About Your Grades

Any writing professor worth his or her salt will write ample notes on your turned-in work. Your writing professor will comment upon what you have done well and what you need to do in the future. Be prepared to see a lot of handwriting on your returned paper, no matter what grade your paper has received. A writing professor's handwritten notes demonstrate real interest in your progress as a beginning writer. In fact, a student ought to be worried more by a lack of notes than too many notes.

Most students, having read their writing professor's notes carefully, will agree with the grades their writing professor has assigned to their work. Other students will nevertheless seek further clarification. Your writing professor will be happy to discuss your paper's grade with you; however, be sure to approach this conversation in the spirit of illumination, and not manipulation. There are some manipulative statements that are never to be spoken during a grade-related conversation with your writing professor. The following statements will persuade your writing professor to believe you are interested much more in milking a grade than in improving as a beginning writer:

- "[But] my high school English teacher said I was the best writer he / she ever had."
- "[But] I need an A to keep my scholarship."
- "[But] I'll fail out of school if I do not pass your class."
- "[But] I am planning to graduate at the end of this semester."
- "[But] I tried really hard."
- "[But] I really like your class."
- "[But] all of my friends got A's. Why didn't I?"
- "[But] you know I am a procrastinator."
- "[But] you're my favorite professor."

The problem with these statements is they attempt to shift responsibility from the student to the writing professor; moreover, these statements play cheaply on the writing professor's emotions.

What Are The Best Paper Topics?

Choosing the best paper topic is simple when a student knows how professional writers choose their own subject matter. Professional writers know the value of originality; their work is much more likely to be published if it creates or redirects public discussion. Professional writers center their trade on exciting their readership, and they make a point of knowing when a topic has become stale. Your writing professor is an avid reader. Like the professional writer, your writing professor has little desire to revisit a tired subject. The student who chooses a paper's topic carefully is that much more likely to be regarded by his or her writing professor as capable.

The student who selects something seen on the news as a topic is likely making a grave mistake. Media today tend to play it safe: few truly original news stories are presented anymore; a number of websites and television networks opt to cover the same events for the sake of ratings. Choosing a topic you have seen on a blog or on the nightly news makes you appear more as a follower than as a leader, and your topic will appear prepackaged. Then again, a student who chooses a "controversial" topic for the sake of creating reader interest is equally misguided as the student likely ends up writing a paper that states the obvious. Many of today's so-called controversies are actually commonplaces. Newsflash: "Abortion is controversial!" "Some athletes use steroids!" "War is unpopular!" "Gun control laws are problematic!" "Some people want to legalize marijuana!" "Anorexia is an eating disorder!" The list goes on. It is much better for you to start from as an original place as possible. Below I suggest five paths to an original topic, with the first and second paths indicative of work belonging to the most creative writers:

1. You introduce a topic that has not appeared in print before.
2. You introduce a topic that addresses an unforeseen problem.
3. You introduce a topic that has appeared in print only very rarely.
4. You introduce a topic that addresses a known problem.
5. You introduce a topic that has appeared in print recently, but your argument will contradict common assumptions related to the topic.

Even a student who has been assigned a topic can write with originality. When a writing professor gives you a topic, he or she wants to see what you can do with it. If you do not shadow the ideas belonging to those who have written on the topic before you, and if you avoid dwelling upon the topic's most common arguments, you will show your writing professor you are capable of thinking for yourself.

Just as a fresh paper topic will help a student stand out as a scholar, a stale paper topic will render a student invisible as a scholar. There are five paths to stale paper topics:

1.   You introduce a topic that is seen commonly in the media.
2.   You introduce a topic that is based on the obvious.
3.   You introduce a topic that is based on an either / or or a black / white proposition.
4.   You introduce a topic that has no hope of being defended.
5.   You introduce a topic that merely reproduces another writer's research.

A student who has chosen a stale topic is a student who has fallen into temptation. We live in a world given to celebrity, and it is not uncommon for Americans to attempt to emulate the rhetorics and interests belonging to their favorite celebrities. In recent years, for example, writing professors have been able to identify from among their students fans of movie director Michael Moore and radio talk show host Rush Limbaugh. How? These fans have openly used their written assignments to ape or mimic the rhetorics and interests of their favorite celebrities. By attempting to be little Moores and Limbaughs, these students have wasted important opportunities to become known for their own rhetorics, to put forth their own interests.

Other paper topics seen by writing professors as dead on arrival involve the supernatural. Topics based on the supernatural tend to suggest limiting, circular arguments will follow. That is, if a student believes his or her holy book or belief system cannot possibly be open to debate, the student will see little need to defend his or her point of view, even if the student's public is for the most part secular. Thus, rhetoric's most important goal, persuasion of the public, will likely not take place.

What Is Research?

Research is careful, thorough study of a given topic. A researcher is one who performs research. Research can be primary, whereby the researcher collects new data or information, secondary, whereby the researcher collects data or information gathered originally by another researcher, or it can be a combination of primary and secondary data. Moreover, research can be quantitative (based on statistics) or qualitative (based on description), or it can be a combination of quantitative and qualitative methodologies. A methodology is a formal approach to research.

Professional researchers tend to assign different values to the kinds of data and to the various research methodologies. Data are judged upon their originality, timeliness, and detail. For instance, primary data are held in a higher regard than secondary data because primary data are gathered first-hand by the researcher, and secondary data consist of the gathered work of others. Primary data are also considered more current because they are gathered specifically for a new study, while secondary data belong to studies published earlier. In regard to the comparative virtues of research methodologies, quantitative or statistical work offers the researcher a large sample of thin descriptors (think surveys), and qualitative or descriptive work offers the researcher a small sample of thick descriptors (think open-ended interviews).

Most students entering university bring with them a basic understanding of secondary research; in high school, students were asked by their English teachers to place quoted materials in their term papers. Your writing professor will pick up where your high school English teacher left off, but with one difference. Once you have mastered secondary research, your writing professor will introduce primary research (e.g. survey and interview) to you.

Good research papers include primary and secondary research. Primary research offers your paper the terrific benefit of original data and the unique opportunity to be the first to analyze it. In this way, your public is compelled to pay close attention to your writing; the knowledge within your paper simply did not exist prior to your analysis. Secondary research lends your paper much-needed depth. A thorough understanding of your topic allows you to state for your public exactly what is known about your topic. The more closely you reveal your topic's relevant issues and understated details, the more your public will see you as an expert. Most significantly, the more you expose flaws in existing research, the more your public will see you as a useful problem solver. Together, primary and secondary research balances your paper. Primary research allows you to go out on a limb, but secondary research secures you to an academic community. Likewise, the originality of primary research keeps you from blandly restating what is known by an academic community.

Although the fruits of primary and secondary research are useful to a paper, you are to remember data are to be incorporated sparingly. In fact, quoted materials should make up no more than ten percent of any paper. You are to remember quoted materials lend support to a point you are making; quoted materials do not make your point for you. Remember also, there is an art to incorporating quoted materials into your paper; they are not to be placed just anywhere. Rather, quoted materials are to be placed where they will do the most good for your argument. Moreover, each quote is to be introduced by at least one sentence, and explained by at least one sentence.

Why Grammar Matters

Until 1905, there existed in China a particularly slow manner of execution known as *língchí*, translated as "death by 1,000 cuts." As the punishment's name suggests, the convicted individual was made to linger until the executioner had bled the individual fully. Many writing professors describe student papers that have suffered mightily under the red pen as having "died by 1,000 cuts." Whether or not such exaggerated description speaks to the writing professors' taste for dark humor, their fairly morbid portrayal says much about the real dangers to student writing posed by incorrect grammar usage. I can attest to this last point. As a writing professor, I have seen more papers fail as a result of poor grammar than poor argument.

A number of thoughtful students will bring to their drafts critical imagination and developed argument. Student problems with grammar, however, tend to be common. Thus, writing professors often find themselves worrying about their students' grammar more than their students' content. True enough, a lack of imagination and a rubbery argument will doom any paper, but when you think about it, content problems can be remedied fairly easily with a professor-student meeting or two. Grammar problems, on the other hand, appear to be much more stubborn because their elimination may require several semesters of dedicated effort. Easily flowing grammar allows your public to devote its entire attention to the point you are making. Jerking grammar, however, forces your public to shift its attention away from the point you want to make, and onto what you are trying to say.

What Office Hours Can Do For You

Colleges and universities place such a high value on constructive professor-student relationships that all schools require their faculty members to hold office hours. Office hours are set times during the week when your professors make themselves available to you exclusively. A scheduling conflict with a professor's office hours is almost never an issue because your professor will gladly set an alternative appointment at a time convenient for both of you.

Office hours are what you make of them; the important thing is you make frequent use of them. Some students visit their writing professor to seek clarification of an assignment's instructions. Your writing professor knows students who are made comfortable with an assignment are much more likely to produce better work, and consequently, achieve much higher grades. Other students will attend their writing professor's office hours to seek help with determining a paper's topic and an appropriate thesis statement. As stated earlier in this chapter, your writing professor is a professional writer and rhetorician. He or she will suggest to you what topic and argument choices are forward-looking, commonplace, and stale. Yet other students will want help with research. Again, no problem there as your writing professor is a professional researcher, too.

A student may think a writing professor's office hours are wholly for one-on-one writing tutorials, but that student would be incorrect. Many students, in fact, use office hours to simply visit with their writing professors. One cannot overemphasize the value of knowing one's writing professor personally. The sooner a student views a writing professor as a friendly colleague, the sooner the student will lose what remains of some people's infantile fear of teachers. It is unfortunate, but as a result of misguided socialization, a few students will absolutely refuse to speak to, or seek help from, their writing professors. Next, it is much easier for your writing professor to help you if your writing professor knows you. This is not to suggest your writing professor will show favoritism toward you; rather, a writing professor can more readily assist a student when a student's strengths and weaknesses as a beginning writer are not sadly kept a mystery. Lastly, your writing professor has made it through college writing successfully; visiting your writing professor's office hours will give you the opportunity to pick his or her brain for tricks of the trade.

Emailing Your Writing Professor

Emailing your writing professor can be a useful activity if you go about it intelligently. Your writing professor receives between 100 and 200 emails weekly. In order to keep your message from getting lost in the fray, avoid the common student mistake of forgetting to include your name in your message. Further, absolutely nothing will make you appear to be a mallrat more quickly than using Text Speak (for instance: "Can I c ur notes b/c my g/f 8 mine?"). Further still, if you have been absent from class, never ask your writing professor

"Did we cover anything important today?" My usual response to such a question is, "No, we sat on our hands."

The Writing Center, Your Best Friend

Most English departments maintain writing centers. A writing center is an office that offers free, one-on-one help to any student, with any paper, assigned in any class. Some writing centers tackle ancillary kinds of writing, such as cover letters, resumes, and scholarship applications, as well. Writing centers are usually staffed by trained student consultants, and headed by a director, who is more likely than not a writing professor. A writing center's chief missions are to help students with argument construction and navigation of the writing process (i.e. prewriting, writing, and revision). Other writing center missions include grammar and citation-related tutoring. A writing center is not a dry cleaning business, whereby staff "clean up" student papers. Rather, a writing center's consultants are more akin to trainers, who impart fundamental skills to interested learners.

In short, writing centers have one purpose: to help strengthen students' writing abilities. Past students of mine who have made frequent use of this service a regular practice routinely outscored students who did not make use of this service.

Plagiarism, Your Mortal Enemy

Plagiarism is a type of theft whereby a dishonest student attempts to pass off the writing and ideas belonging to another author as the student's own work. Writing professors typically have five options when they uncover student plagiarism. The writing professor may fail the plagiarized paper, and allow the student to remain in class, or the writing professor may give the student a failing grade for the entire course. Likewise, the writing professor may send the student to student court, and allow the student court to decide an appropriate punishment, or the writing professor may ask the student court to expel the student from university. Then again, the writing professor may apply a combination of the four options mentioned above. In any event, a student found guilty of having plagiarized will carry the reputation of a thief; plagiarism is that serious of a crime. Plagiarism's stigma is such that most students who have plagiarized are made to give up any hope of graduate school. A school does not like a thief in its midst.

Students who attempt to plagiarize are not master thieves by any means; in fact, a writing professor can spot plagiarism easily. Most students tend to write at their level. That is to say, a freshman's writing will often resemble the writing of other freshmen. A freshman's writing, no matter how advanced a writer he or she is, will not resemble writing belonging to a professional writer. A red flag appears whenever a writing professor reads work comparable to his or her own. Then there is cutting and pasting from the Internet, another red flag; few plagiarists bother to even make sure the font of the stolen works jibe with those of their papers.

Plagiarism is doubly tragic. First, plagiarism destroys forever a writing professor's trust in you. Next, plagiarism is completely avoidable. Unintentional plagiarism will not occur if you cite every word you did not write, and every idea you did not think up yourself. Most students who plagiarize intentionally do so because they waited far too long to begin their projects.

What You Will Take From This Book

In Chapter 1, "How to Start a Paper," attention is given to the fundamentals of topic and argument creation: inventio, tempus, stasis, thesis, counter-thesis, ethos, logos, and pathos. I suggest the student's task of preparing an argument is similar to a prosecutor's pretrial work; arguing well depends upon anticipating any possible question. Chapter 1 finds the student compared to a boxer entering the ring. A student who does not know how to prepare an argument's defense will be knocked out rhetorically in short order.

Chapter 2, "How to Build a Paper," starts with a review of grammar; a student who does not know how to employ language to full effect will not be understood, and the student will fail to be persuasive. Then, after I give attention to paragraph development, the student will be introduced to citing researched materials and two citation styles, American Psychological Association (APA) and Modern Language Association (MLA). Students who do not know how to cite researched materials correctly risk plagiarizing work belonging to others.

Chapter 3, "How to Revise a Paper," emphasizes revision's leading position within the writing process. Self-critical revision is the hallmark of a professional writer, and a student would do well to know the first draft of a research paper is never acceptable. Revision strategies are offered here. Chapter 3 ends with an array of revision workshop ideas.

Chapter 4, "Select Examples of Student Writing" provides two representative examples of student writing: "Meaningful lives of the undead: A deeper look into the substantiveness of the modern gothic lifestyle", a paper based on secondary research, and "Disabling misconceptions: A study on the dating practices of physically disabled women and able-bodied men", a paper based on primary and secondary research.

Chapter 1
How to Start a Paper

"Without leaps of imagination, or dreaming, we lose the excitement of possibilities. Dreaming, after all, is a form of planning."
Gloria Steinem

Trial By Fire

It is the first day of the semester, and you are reading your writing class' syllabus. You notice a paper is due in five weeks. The idea of writing is enough to frighten you, but being asked to come up with a college-level paper in about a month is, well, you think that is the stuff nightmares are made of. So, what are you going to do?

You will not ask your writing professor when to begin your paper. Your writing professor assumes go-ahead is given for all assignments once the class' syllabi are handed out on the first day of the semester. Moreover, once your writing professor has introduced an assignment to your class formally, do not expect your writing professor to remind you of the paper's due date, or to even ask if you are working on the paper. Unlike a high school English teacher, a university writing professor views you as an adult. The last thing your writing professor wants to do is to insult an adult with a redundant warning to handle adult responsibilities correctly. In short, you will find your writing professor is much different than your high school English teacher; the sooner you understand university is not high school, the better.

Rest assured; your writing professor does not assume you enter Freshman Composition already able to write at college-level. There would be little point in taking the class if you did. Rather, the first thing your writing professor expects you to do after receiving an assignment is to begin planning the paper. Your writing professor expects you to begin this planning by employing a uniquely human faculty you have brought with you from grade school, your imagination. Imagination is the ability to create mental images or ideas of what is not present; more generally, imagination is your brain's power to envision, confront and work out difficulties. Think back to when you were a child. Imagination came easily to you because it was so much fun to contradict reality: a living room sofa became a pirate ship, and the blue shag carpet became a shark-infested ocean. Woe to him or her who could not jump from the ship to the loveseat island! You have not lost your imagination with age; on the contrary, your imagination still resides in your brain. However, because an adult's imagination is used most frequently to come up with creative solutions for everyday problems (e.g. "How am I going to make my car payment?"), and less frequently for pure fun, you likely see imagination as belonging to the distant past. In the context of paper planning, imagination is used to contradict reality (e.g. "What is a new way to think about my topic?"), and as a problem-solving mechanism (e.g. "What is the best way to persuade others to act upon my point of view?).

Inventio

Inventio, a Latin word meaning invention or discovery, refers to a student's methodical search for arguments, and is of first importance to your paper planning. As a theoretical concept, inventio reminds the student that an argument's success or failure depends largely on the student's ability to imagine or foresee any possible question the public may have. The more you anticipate public concern in your writing, the more persuasive your argument will be. It is seldom the known question that sinks a student's argument; rather, it is the question that has not been considered that makes a student's argument seem half-baked, and as a result, appear untrustworthy.

When applied as a student's tool, inventio's beauty is found in its timelessness. Consisting of a series of open-ended questions, you can carry inventio from paper to paper and from semester to semester. Mastering inventio is simply a matter of committing important questions to your memory, and recalling these questions when you first plan a new paper. As a search for arguments, inventio moves from basic to complex questions and from basic to complex rhetorical maneuvers. Inventio's ten most basic questions include:

1. What is one idea not yet known about your topic?
   a. Why is your public unaware of this idea?
2. What will this idea mean to your public?
   a. How will your public receive this idea?
3. What does your public already know about your topic?
   a. Who stands to benefit from the introduction of your idea?
4. What are you arguing?
   a. How will your public be impacted by your argument?
5. What words are most important to your argument and how do you define these words?
   a. Do you or others define these words?

Within these ten questions three concerns become apparent: your argument's originality, your argument's socio-centric approach, and the origin of the words your argument will depend on. Earlier in this book I suggested an argument's originality is paramount; the student who chooses a paper's topic with originality in mind is that much more likely to be regarded by his or her writing professor as capable. Next, the student is to remember one does not write a paper for oneself; a paper is neither a diary entry, nor a confessional blog. Rather, one writes to affect positive change in a public's thinking. Last, a student's taxonomy, his or her word and definition choices, will mark the student as a trendsetter or as a member of a school of thought. A school of thought consists of people who share the same opinions, follow the same philosophy, or belong to the same cultural, social, or political movements. Given membership into most schools of thought is based on loyalty to similar ideas, taxonomies that balance trend-setting and established views are fairly uncommon. That is to say, how many communist capitalists do you know?

Speaking of word choice, and moving inventio along from basic to complex questions, let us turn our attention to questions that deconstruct a student's taxonomy. To deconstruct a taxonomy is to expose the inexact meaning of words, whereby the taxonomy's words appear to suggest many definitions that are often in disagreement with one another. Words are not merely chosen by a student from a dictionary or thesaurus. Rather, deconstruction suggests words are what are left of long-standing prejudices, quarrels, dreams, and hierarchies, as evidenced by the friction and uncertainty expressed by, for instance, male and female, black and white, old and young, or gay and straight. Inventio, then, assists a student's deconstructive reading; the 12 questions below allow you to pay close attention to your taxonomy's words' meanings.

1. How many definitions do your taxonomy's words have?
2. What uncertainties are exposed by your definitions?
3. What are the most socially popular definitions?
4. What are the least socially popular definitions?
5. Who is most likely to use your definitions?
6. Who is least likely to use your taxonomy's words?
7. Who should not use your taxonomy's words?
8. What social prejudices are contained in your definitions?
9. What social conflicts are exposed by your definitions?
10. What social hopes or dreams are exposed by your definitions?
11. What social power structures are exposed by your definitions?
12. What social tensions are exposed by your definitions?

A student who invests the time to discover the actual and perceived meanings of words important to a paper demonstrates good planning; moreover, such planning keeps the student from confusing the public unnecessarily. Knowing what a word can mean to the public compels you to choose and apply the definition most effective for your purpose; your word knowledge can keep your public on track. Say, for instance, you are writing about gender's role in the

Freshman Composition classroom. As it stands today, "gender" may be defined at least three ways. Complicating matters is the fact each of these definitions relates somewhat to the aforementioned Freshman Composition classroom. For example, gender can refer simply to the biological sex (i.e. male or female) of the students belonging to the Freshman Composition classroom you speak of. However, gender can refer also to the socialization (i.e. gender roles and sexual identity) expressed in the Freshman Composition classroom. Gender can lastly refer to the application of grammatical categories (i.e. masculine and feminine) learned in the Freshman Composition classroom. Thus, without planning to clarify your definition early in your paper, you will leave your public to infer what exactly you mean by gender. Leaving your public to decide what you mean in a paper is quite a dangerous thing to do as your public demands strict attention to detail. Your public expects you to be an expert on your paper's subject, and without such expertise you will come off as a lightweight.

Inventio can take your paper planning even farther. In fact, knowing the right questions to ask can help you plan for a paper in its entirety. Put simply, inventio removes much of the guess work from your writing process; no longer will you assume writing a paper involves sitting at a computer and hoping one idea will follow another. Inventio reminds us writing is a deliberate act. Professional writers are able to produce several pages of text a week because they are organized. They approach their computers knowing what they will write, and where they will write it. I use the following inventio-inspired list of questions whenever I plan a paper (Yes, professors write papers. They stay sharp by presenting their work at academic conferences.). From these questions I develop sentences and paragraphs; the choice is mine. Please note this template addresses primary and secondary research. If your paper uses secondary research only, disregard the Method and Results portion.

Introduction

1. What is the need for my argument?
   a. How does this project serve the community?

   b. What community does this project serve?
2. What is the significance of my argument?
   a. What do I hope to accomplish with my argument?
   b. Who will resist my argument?
   c. What impact will this resistance have upon my argument?
3. What is the history of my argument?
   a. Am I saying anything new?
   b. Am I continuing an academic conversation?
4. How do I define the terms most important to my argument?
   a. Am I saying anything new?
   b. Do my definitions reflect membership in a school of thought?
5. What prejudice do I bring to this argument?
   a. What brought me to this topic?
   b. What do I hope to gain if my argument is persuasive?
   c. Do I speak for a community?

Literature Review

1. What does my public already know about my topic?
   a. Do different schools of thought interpret this information differently?
2. What are my topic's most relevant details?
   a. Why are these details the most important?
   b. Which scholars would disagree with me?
   c. Which scholars would agree with me?
3. What are my topic's underlying details?
   a. Do these underlying details add depth to my argument?
   b. How were these underlying details discovered?
4. What limitations are contained in my secondary research materials?
   a. What do these limitations mean to my argument?

b.   How may I turn limitations in others' research into opportunities for my argument?

c.   How does my argument serve as a remedy to these preexisting limitations?

Method and Results

1.   Which volunteers participated in my study?
     a.   What is the volunteers' demographic information?
2.   What measures and equipment were used to collect primary data?
     a.   How do I justify each survey and interview question?
          i.   Do my questions borrow from previous primary research?
     b.   What information did each survey and interview question hope to collect?
3.   How did I collect my primary data?
4.   How do I summarize my primary data?

Discussion

1.   Were my initial beliefs supported, challenged, or changed by my collected research?
     a.   In what ways?
2.   How does my argument fit in with published arguments?
     a.   To what extent does my argument stand alone?
3.   How well can my findings be applied to an actual setting?
     a.   Does my argument remain theoretical?
          i.   Why?
4.   What limitations are found in my study?
     a.   What implications do these limitations present?
5.   What should future research projects on the same subject look like?

Inventio is an art. A student who is willing to harness the power of his or her imagination will master this art much sooner than the student who is less willing, or is unable, to look beyond immediate reality. Inventio compels the student to move away from superficial or shallow thinking when searching for arguments and planning a paper; inventio's nature is to challenge the status quo.

Tempus

Tempus is a Latin word for time. Whereas inventio helps a student search for original arguments, and assists in planning a paper's content, tempus helps a student judge how timely an argument is. In our case, timely refers to introducing an argument *ad tempus*, at the most correct moment. Further, the importance of your argument's timeliness cannot be overstated; your decision when to introduce an argument will make you appear to your public as a leader, a follower, or as a dinosaur. Again, viewing things as your writing professor would proves useful.

Your writing professor does not confuse timeliness with currency. Currency is a label suggesting the immediate, but passing, value of fashionable topics, as in "this news story has currency." The trouble with fashionable topics is they soon become cliché. It is the unfortunate habit of today's media to converge upon a topic in what is called a news cycle until the public is made wholly tired with the subject. If, for instance, ESPN breaks a story about pitcher Joe Smith using steroids, you can bet almost every local sports reporter will cover the same story until a new topic becomes fashionable. Moreover, if you take the medias' lead, and make the aforementioned Joe Smith's steroid use the topic of your paper, you risk handing your writing professor a stale project. This is especially true if the media have already moved on to another news cycle. In short, tempus demands that you do not hitch your argument to other writers' stars.

Timeliness, on the other hand, speaks to an opportune event, as in "it is high time someone wrote about this." An argument that introduces a completely new idea to the public is almost always seen as well-timed for the simple reason the new idea offers a welcome alternative to the stale topics that have flooded the marketplace. If other writers then choose to take your lead, and ape your topic, so be it; they would be following you, a trend setter. Almost as timely as a student's choice to reshape public interest is the student's choice to redirect public interest. For example, if the media are speaking continuously about a school shooting, and dredge up the inevitable gun control debate, you would do well to present an opposite discussion, and speak of the prevalence of healthy student relationships and how violence among Americans is exaggerated often. Yes, your choice to redirect public interest would make you a part of a current discussion, but few of your critics could accuse you of following the pack blindly. Tempus favors the student who sets or alters the public's agenda.

Some topics possess neither timeliness, nor currency, yet a few misguided students will flock to these topics every semester. The subject of anorexia comes to mind. In regard to anorexia, most of the public already knows it is an eating-related, control-based psychological disorder, which is associated most commonly with teenagers, that it affects males and females, and that it is treated with long-term psychiatric counseling. Unless a student who chooses anorexia as a topic plans to propose a truly fresh idea, such as a revolutionary treatment for the disease, the student will merely cover the same ground others ventured into 30-odd years ago. A student might suggest to a writing professor that anorexia ought to be written about as a means of raising public awareness, but like drunk driving, teen pregnancy, and drug abuse, the subject has saturated the marketplace in the form of classroom lectures, television commercials, and *After School Specials* for decades. Tempus is more forward-looking than backward-looking.

A word of caution is in order. The strong emphasis I place on an idea's timeliness and originality does not suggest a student ought to disregard the value of secondary or book research. On the contrary, the more knowledgeable a student makes him or herself on a topic, the more trust the public will place in the student's argument. Further, once a student has used secondary research to learn what was been said about a topic, the student will be far less likely to mimic ideas belonging to others.

The following tempus-based checklist will help you judge your topic's timeliness and your argument's originality:

- Your idea came to you completely on your own.
  (Most timely and original)
- Your idea came to you as a response to something you heard in a class.
- Your idea came to you as a response to something you read in a book.
- Your idea came to you as a response to something you read in a journal.
- Your idea came to you as a response to something you read in a magazine.
- Your idea came to you as a response to something you heard or read on the Internet, news, radio, or television.
  (Least timely and original)

Note what appears to be the checklist's unusual progression: younger media products are assigned lower positions than older media products, and unpublished ideas place higher than published ideas. This is in keeping with tempus. You may have first heard of a subject on yesterday's evening news, but so did the world. And in the five weeks you are given to write a paper, the subject might very well have become old news. However, information contained in books is different than the information contained in news broadcasts. Most news broadcasts attempt to capture specific moments in time; they have shelf lives. Most books, on the other hand, attempt to speak to whole subjects; they are meant to be timeless. Further still, while unpublished ideas have yet to meet with the academic scrutiny published materials receive, their comparative freshness suggests new directions of thought.

Stasis

Stasis, a Greek word meaning standing still, refers to the opinion upon which an argument is built. Stasis is also another word for standpoint. Because each of us expresses many standpoints in our daily lives, stasis can reflect a trivial point of view, as in "I like pizza with mushrooms," or stasis can reflect a serious point of view, as in "No child should be allowed to starve." The important thing to remember is that stasis is central to the development of your paper's argument. The result of not knowing exactly where you stand on an issue during the planning of your work is an essay that lacks focus.

Expressing your point of view sounds like an easy thing to do, and it is, because all you have to do is make up your mind and communicate. However, far too many students today view boredom or apathy within the university classroom as part of being fashionably jaded. These otherwise intelligent people will pretend not to have opinions in front of their classmates and professors in a naïve effort to appear worldly or sophisticated. Sadly for these students, writing professors view the apathetic as immature and awkward, especially if apathy finds its way into professor-student conversations. Think of it this way: your writing professor has eyes and ears; he or she sees students talking with one another before and after class, and hears them debating everything from the price of blank compact disks to whether or not a mutual acquaintance should enter a rehab program for prescription drug addiction. Because your writing professor has heard you expressing your point of view to others before, choosing to tell your writing professor, "I don't know what interests me," or "I have no opinions," while planning your paper together will make you appear a ninny rather quickly.

A stasis is viewed best as an argument in embryonic form, a starting point. Your job is to grow your stasis into a thesis. In other words, you are to develop your point of view into a definitive statement that will be made persuasive to your public through the support you give it later on in your paper's content. A stasis is an argument's skeleton in need of muscles, ligaments, and tendons. The five questions below will help you to give flesh to your point of view:

1. What are the facts?
    a. Did something occur?
    b. Will something occur?

2. What is to be defined?
   a. What occurred?
      i. What is the best way to describe the occurrence?
      ii. How should the occurrence not be described?
   b. Do people interpret what occurred differently?
      i. Who interprets what occurred differently?
      ii. Who interprets what occurred similarly?
   c. What will occur?
      i. What is the best way to describe this future occurrence?
      ii. How should this future occurrence not be described?
   d. Do people interpret your premonition differently?
      i. Who interprets your premonition differently?
      ii. Who interprets your premonition similarly?
3. What are the causes and effects?
   a. What led to this occurrence?
   b. What are the results of this occurrence?
   c. What will lead to this occurrence?
   d. What will the results of this occurrence be?
4. What is the significance?
   a. Was the occurrence good or bad?
   b. Will this occurrence be good or bad?
   c. Was the occurrence useful or not useful?
   d. Will this occurrence be useful or not useful?
   e. Was the occurrence fair or unfair?
   f. Will this occurrence be fair or unfair?
5. What are future considerations?
   a. What should be done?
   b. What should not be done?

The road from stasis to thesis is paved with detail. In regard to paper planning, stasis is useful for two reasons. First, as I have suggested above, stasis provides you with much-needed direction when you plan your paper; you create a path you can stick to when you determine your point of view early. Many writing professors, in fact, refer to a stasis as a preliminary or "working" thesis. Next, stasis is a tool everyone, from the beginning writer to the veteran author, carries with them; you have your opinions, and I have mine. The trick is to remember a stasis is an undeveloped thesis. A thesis is, conversely, a detailed stasis. You may, for example, approach a writing assignment with the stasis, "Madonna's movies suck," but think how much easier your point of view would be to defend with a thesis statement, like, "Madonna's formulaic movies are of low quality because they possess neither plot development, nor believable characters." Yes, your point of view, "Madonna's movies suck" is emphatic, and it suggests your paper will argue the singer's movies are of low quality, but only in a very general sense; "suck" as used here speaks of nothing specific. On the other hand, words found in the example thesis, "formulaic," "low quality," "plot development," and "believable characters" give you ammunition for at least four paragraphs. Again, writing professors regard a stasis as a first step to a thesis.

Thesis

Thesis is a Greek word for position; when your writing professor speaks of a "thesis statement" he or she is referring to a position statement. The word has come to mean an essential, precise, guiding sentence that will be defended in each of your paper's paragraphs. The thesis' traditional home is within a paper's first paragraph, though there is some debate among writing professors as to whether a thesis should begin or end this introductory paragraph (it is similar to the question of choosing to throw a punch as soon as the first boxing bell rings or making sure to throw a final, devastating punch at the end of the first round). In any event, a paper without a thesis is like an athlete with two blown knees: neither will move forward quickly; rather, both will ramble along painfully, if at all. You have likely been made aware of thesis in high school English, but this important subject bears review. I describe the review below as "Thesis' Ten Commandments."

1. A thesis statement will not end with a question mark. Remember, you are making an explicit statement, and not asking a question.

2. A thesis statement will not include phrases, such as "I think," "I feel," or "I believe" because such phrases are redundant. You were the one to come up with the argument; who else would your thoughts, feelings, or beliefs belong to?

3. A thesis statement will not include the unnecessary phrase, "I argue that." A thesis *is* an argument. That you have chosen to center your paper on a particular argument is enough to suggest you are, in fact, arguing the point.

4. A thesis statement will not include a quote. Borrowed ideas do not make the writer's point for him or her. Quoted materials are employed by a writer well into a paper to lend support to the point he or she is making, or to contradict ideas belonging to others.

5. A thesis statement will not include vague language. A thesis sums up your argument in one sentence, so it is important your thesis' wording is as specific as possible.

6. A thesis statement will contain as many words from your taxonomy as possible. Given the importance your public assigns to detail, it is critical your thesis suggests to your public what key words and phrases will guide your paper.

7. A thesis statement will contain an original point. Knowing what other authors have already said about your topic will keep you from acting the parrot in your thesis.

8. A thesis statement will contain momentum. Thesis is an offensive play; you use it to forward your idea. You want your argument to be able to move beyond your first paragraph, your paper's line of scrimmage. Therefore, your thesis is to avoid limiting circular arguments, as in "Chicken wings taste good because they are delicious."

9. A thesis statement will contain enough ammunition for several paragraphs. Your thesis should be broad enough to allow each of your paragraphs to expand your argument.

10.   A thesis statement will contain hope. Bringing a subject up without offering a practical solution is whining. That said, your thesis will mention problem and solution.

If you take anything from our thesis review, take this: the more original your argument is, the more your public will have to pay attention to what you have written. Further, your public will be much less able to refute your unique idea as you will have made yourself an authority on the matter. At best, you will have introduced an idea few have considered before. Next best is you will have redirected an on-going conversation. In either case, you will have placed all of your public's eyes on you, and as you will learn later in this chapter, a writer's ethos, his or her reputation, means almost everything.

Counter-thesis

Counter-thesis is another word for counter-argument, and both denote an opposing point of view. You are to give as much attention to counter-thesis as you would thesis. Your writing professor will ask you to consider two principal varieties of counter-theses when you plan your paper: arguments that contradict your point of view and your arguments that contradict the points of view held by other authors. Your writing professor's request is based on the idea there is at least one counter-thesis for every thesis, from explicit refutations to subtle corrections. For example, an explicit refutation:

<u>Cold pizza tastes good in the morning.</u>
Cold pizza does not taste good in the morning.

By adding the adjective "not" to the first sentence, one comes up with a very basic counter-thesis, a dichotomy. It is a simple-enough proposition. Much more interesting is the following subtle correction I take from a conversation I had with one of my graduate assistants. Note the lovely nuance found in her response (below) to my thesis (above):

<u>Dogs go to Heaven.</u>
No place can be called Heaven if it does not have dogs.

What I like particularly about my graduate assistant's counter-thesis is she made her argument her own. Yes, both thesis and counter-thesis talk about dogs and Heaven, but notice how she transformed my idea (i.e. "Dogs go to Heaven") by redefining the very nature of Heaven (i.e. "No place can be called Heaven *if*..."). I left myself open for her counter-punch when I took the nature of Heaven for granted. Another two examples will prove especially useful. Below are popular examples I give my students whenever the subjects of ethnicity and poverty come up in my classroom:

<u>African American students keep to themselves.</u>
Caucasian students need to be more welcoming to members of other cultures.

<u>Residents of New Orleans should have left the city when warned of Hurricane Katrina's danger.</u>
Given New Orleans' exceeding poverty, many citizens simply did not have the hundreds, perhaps thousands, of dollars needed to relocate when warned of Hurricane Katrina's danger.

Talk about a couple of one-two punches! These last two examples of counter-theses are striking for a few reasons. First, both counter-theses flip the script; the counter-theses do away quickly with the simplistic, implied stereotypes contained in the theses (e.g. African Americans prefer only each other's company; southerners were too dumb to move out of the way of a dangerous storm). Second, because both counter-theses are centered upon sympathetic logic, and not mere opinion like the two theses, the counter-theses will appear to the public as more reasonable, more persuasive arguments. The counter-theses shift accountability from minority groups historically without access to social power to majority groups historically with access to social power. These counter-theses remind the public it is the majority white students' responsibility to be inclusive, and that wealthier individuals are to remember poorer individuals have far fewer options. In short, counter-thesis demands mental agility. A student who does think on his or her feet when planning a thesis will be knocked out rhetorically by another's solid counter-thesis.

Many students take themselves and their ideas far too seriously. Today's student often appears unwilling to engage in the withering self-criticism demanded by a thorough recognition of counter-thesis. This general unwillingness to consider arguments that contradict the student's own point of view may be the result of having been raised with the now popular, but overly optimistic belief that each person is extraordinary, a thing like no other, beyond reproach. Then again, the problem of the overfed ego also appears to be culture-wide in America; it extends from little league "competitions," where scores are not kept so every participant is made a "winner," to self-affirming t-shirts that proclaim such statements as, "I look forward to non-judgment day." In other words, and unfortunately for the student raised to see him or herself as above judgment, the study of counter-thesis is based partly on the severe judgment of the student's point of view.

A well written thesis is like armor without gaps. The more thoughtful your thesis is, the less penetrating a counter-thesis will be. Conversely, every place your thesis leaves room for a counter-argument is another opportunity for your public to mistrust you; too much mistrust on your public's part and your thesis will lie on the arena floor wounded mortally. When your writing professor plays devil's advocate at a professor-student meeting, and pokes holes in your thesis unmercifully, he or she is actually doing you and your paper a great favor. Remember, your primary goal as a writer is persuasion of your public, and not self-gratification. A writer who knows and appeals to the needs of his or her public is more likely to persuade readers to think, to feel, or to do as the writer so wishes. In this way, your public's level of comfort with your thesis is much more important than any warm fuzzies going about unquestioned may give you.

You would be correct in thinking my discussion of counter-thesis makes the subject sound like gladiatorial combat. Counter-thesis *is* like gladiatorial combat. You will find countering is indeed a contact sport, and an often bloody one at that, especially when your paper planning brings you to contradicting the points of view held by established authors. Know this: many of the ideas behind what we consider to be today's most important advances (whether they involve thinking, technology, ways of going about life; you name it) have as their catalyst the past's failures. Writers possess a similar catalyst. We write today to correct the incomplete writing belonging to yesterday. If the subject you are tackling has been covered so thoughtfully that an earlier writer is said to have written the final world on the subject, your public will simply have no use for what you have to say. Your ideas will appear redundant. On the other hand, you can make quite a name for yourself if you center your work on exposing and acting upon the limitations contained in less thoughtful research. Every flaw in existing research is an open window of opportunity for you. Thus, counter-thesis is a question of bravery. Are you brave enough to contradict ideas belonging to established writers? Guess what: most established writers were students once, and they entered the arena by challenging prior research, too. Their crowns are now yours to take. Below are four questions related to counter-thesis. You are expected to apply them when you criticize not only ideas belonging to others, but to your own ideas as well.

1.   Who is incorrect?
2.   What is incorrect in the author's writing?
3.   When or where is the author incorrect?
4.   Why or how is the author incorrect?

Like hockey, counter-thesis can be rough, but neither is wholly about checking one's opponent. Hockey and counter-thesis have rules to follow, and there are penalties for those who become too hot headed. Again like hockey, counter-thesis depends on agility; too much unnecessary grappling and both slow down. Fortunately for you, adhering to the following two rules will keep you in the counter-thesis game. Hockey has a whole book of rules to learn.

1.   Never name call. Name-calling is a particularly cheap thing to do in writing because it is too easy. The ancient

Greeks regarded name-callers as biting insects, and your public regards name-calling as hitting below the belt. This rule refers also to insinuation, whereby a writer hints at an opponent's negative quality.

2. Never employ stereotypes. Stereotypes are lazy generalizations, and your public will see you as a lazy writer if you use stereotypes.

Ethos

Ethos, a Greek word meaning character, credibility, and reputation, has come to refer to the shared trustworthiness of a writer and of whatever outside evidence or sources the writer uses to strengthen his or her argument's position. Ethos is a notably hard-won quality, and it can be lost quite easily, for while a writer yearns to create a sense of ethos, it very much remains a quality the writer's public chooses to impart to him or her. In other words, although you may attempt to show yourself as serious, believable, and worthy of respect in your written work, it is squarely up to your public to see you in those terms, or not. You are not "lent" ethos when your writing professor instructs you to write on a subject; rather, you earn ethos when you have shown yourself to be an expert on the subject. Likewise, as your idea becomes tied to it, the outside evidence you choose to support your argument with will either enhance or diminish your ethos in your public's eyes. Evidence must be chosen carefully, and not all evidence is equal; it can be a stone to build with, or a stone that will pull you under. Just as you would not cite Adolph Hitler in an argument promoting interracial love, you should not wish to cite an anonymous website, as the author's ethos is so unclear. For all you know, your best friend's 13-year old brother could have posted the website. Given ethos' elusive nature, it is much better for you to strengthen your argument only with evidence of high ethical value. To be clear, who you are is not as important as what your public takes you to be. Though unfair, perception supersedes reality often. Further, your public will view the evidence you use as an extension of the quality of your thought. Evidence you have gathered from the works of respected authors will likely bring you respect, and evidence you have gathered from disrespected authors will likely bring you disrespect.

This is not to suggest you cannot *attempt* to manipulate the level of ethos your public grants you; anything is possible. On the contrary, persuasion is, after all, an attempt to get your public to think, to feel, or to do as you so wish. Just understand that until you have made a respectable name for yourself, which is not an easy thing to do, your public will view your writing as one of the many voices competing for its limited, often fickle attention. That said, below are three disarming, ethos-related strategies for beginning writers who have yet to develop widely-respected ethoi:

1. Show practicality in your writing. When in doubt, choose to place greater emphasis on material or actual reality and less emphasis on abstract or theoretical reality. Yes, theories have their uses, especially when you are offering future solutions to current problems; however, your public will view you as more down to earth, and most importantly as one of its members, if you show yourself to be fully aware of how things are today from your public's perspective.

2. Show that you have your public's best interests at heart. People tend to be selfish creatures. While your public may be *interested* in the wellbeing of other groups, your public is *concerned* about its own wellbeing. Your writing ought to speak to your public's immediate needs first to gain its attention. Then, speak to your public's long-term needs. Doing so will suggest you care about your public deeply.

3. Show your public you come as a friend. Nobody likes a nag. No matter how boorishly your public behaves, and no matter how much you would like to improve the situation with your argument, it is seldom a good idea to play the scold. Your lack of established ethos has already created a divide between you and your public. It makes little sense to increase this divide, so avoid making your discussion personal. Speak to general perpetrators instead of specific perpetrators. In other words, speak to the whole of your

public, and do not scapegoat anyone. Further, suggest all may share in a brighter future.

A student's ethos suffers most if it becomes apparent the student has not become expert in his or her subject matter during the long course of research. This is why your writing professor will give you so much time to conduct research for major written projects, and why waiting until the last minute to begin such a project can devastate your grade so. I once had a student, who, after he had learned he had received a failing grade on a term paper, exclaimed to me angrily, "But I spent all night writing this!"

"That's the problem," I answered. "I assigned this paper to you 15-weeks ago." This student's problem was a simple one: By wasting the time I had given him for research, he presented an amateurish understanding of his material. Given an expert is much more trustworthy than a novice, I saw this student's superficial work as having little ethos.

Logos

Logos is Greek for word, text, and reason. The term alludes to a fascinating intersection of grammar and meaning, idea and research, and writer's voice and logic. That is to say, whereas grammar requires proper word choice, logos reminds the writer to select the very best word to convey his or her exact meaning. Further, just as an idea drives a paper forward, logos calls upon the paper's writer to incorporate the data or research most able to help substantiate his or her idea. Further still, whereas a writer wishes to make his or her point in a unique way, logos reminds the writer to nevertheless employ a language and a manner of presentation most logical for the writer's public. Then again, logos refers also to bridges between word and figurative language (e.g. metaphor, simile) and word and social context. Think, for instance, of the word, "mother." At heart, "mother" signifies "female parent," but who celebrates Female Parent's Day? No, most of us celebrate Mother's Day. Logos reminds us "mother" obviously means much more to our society than the neutral "female parent." A boy's best friend, after all, is his mother.

A student would be hard pressed to find better logos-related advice than that offered by George Orwell (1946) in his important essay, "Politics and the English Language."[1] So useful was Orwell's advice to me that when I was a student I had taped the following list of six rules to my home computer:

(i)   Never use a metaphor, simile, or other figure of speech which you are used to seeing in print.
(ii)   Never use a long word where a short one will do.
(iii)   If it is possible to cut a word out, always cut it out.
(iv)   Never use the passive voice where you can use the active.
(v)   Never use a foreign phrase, a scientific word, or a jargon word if you can think of an everyday English equivalent.
(vi)   Break any of these rules sooner than say anything out-right barbarous. (pp. 365-6)

Put simply, Orwell is suggesting the more plainly and directly you write, the more your public will understand and trust you. Honest writing, Orwell implies, will further increase the size of your public because most everyone, regardless of their reading levels, will take your meaning. Lastly, few members of your public will be able to call you an unoriginal thinker and writer because you will have refused to let your ideas fall back on clichés. Now, you are probably thinking, if only writing scholars would do as Orwell suggests, and seek divorces from Greek and Latin words!

Just as ethos reminds you to consider your reputation when you plan your paper, logos calls upon you to consider the importance of your word use. Ethos and logos are not unrelated. A poor use of grammar will affect your reputation as a writer negatively. Why should your public trust someone who presents an unclear point of view?

Pathos

Speaking generally, pathos, a Greek word encompassing suffering, passion, and feeling, has come to mean a writer's appeal to his or her public's emotions. More specifically, pathos is an essential, persuasive move meant to arouse a noticeable, specific feeling among the writer's public. To this end, the writer of a sad tale is successful only if he or she compels the public to mist-up or cry, and the writer of a comedic tale is successful only if he or she compels the public to giggle or laugh. The emotional arousal I refer to is most certainly not a given; you are not to take your public's emotional investment in your writing for granted because there is precious little your public has not seen, felt or heard of before. The Internet has seen to that. Rather, pathos suggests it is wholly your responsibility as a writer to move your public to feel something far beyond boredom when it reads your writing.

The rewards of moving your audience to feel emotion are immense. First, a public made emotional is a public made mentally disarmed; a majority of your public is likely to accept and act upon your argument if it trusts you enough to follow your writing to emotional intimacy. Second, if you are capable of creating excitement among your public, your public will perceive you as an exciting writer, and your ethos will benefit. Third, because your public probably views itself as more sophisticated than it actually is, getting it to feel something considered profound will be enough cause for your public to see you as logical, and your logos will be enhanced. The list goes on, but the important thing to remember is humans are emotional animals. Your writing has to appeal as much to the heart as it does to the head.

Nowhere has my discussion appeared more cynical than it has here, but the fact is pathos-influenced arguments are all around us. Is it any mystery why commercials seeking money for starving children appear in great numbers at dinnertime? The charities responsible for these commercials are playing on the emotions surrounding our guilt for having full plates of food. Ever wonder why Disney's movies tend to have mother characters die off? There is no better way to capture a tot's attention than to summon-up his or her desperate fears of separation anxiety. Do not get me started on Sarah McLachlan's ASPCA commercials.

Pathos should be incorporated into your writing with as much precision as possible. It is a matter of planning what specific emotions you want your public to feel, and where to specifically encourage these emotions for greatest persuasive effect. Myself, I prefer to have a pathos-themed outline run parallel to my content outline. Doing so allows me to plan tears and punch lines down to the sentence level.

In the preceding chapter, attention was given to the fundamentals of topic and argument creation. Paper planning was discussed thoroughly, and inventio (invention), tempus (time), stasis (standpoint), thesis (position), counter-thesis (counter-argument), ethos (reputation), logos (reason), and pathos (feeling) were shown to be a student's most useful paper planning-related tools. The next chapter starts with a review of grammar, moves on to a discussion of paragraph development, and concludes with citation instruction.

Chapter 2
How to Build a Paper

"The difference between the almost right word and the right word is really a large matter—it's the difference between the lightning bug and the lightning."

Mark Twain

Brick, Wall, And Ornament

Grammar is important for two reasons. First, grammar helps to organize thought. A student who does not know how to employ language to full effect will not be understood, and the student's paper will fail to be persuasive. In other words, were you to write poorly, your public would be forced to invest the whole of its limited time in attempting to comprehend what you are trying to say. Boredom would then set in among your public, and any interesting point you had to make would be lost to your public's growing sense of frustration with you. Second, grammar lends beauty to your paper. The precision with which you choose and arrange your words is equivalent to grace; the more precise your writing is, the less cumbersome your thinking appears.

Think back to your introduction to logos. Your use of grammar is to be centered on applying the ideal word and the ideal punctuation at the ideal time. Writing professors refer to this application as *le mot juste*, a French phrase meaning the correct word at the correct moment. Gustave Flaubert, my favorite author, once spent an entire month fine-tuning a paragraph. In this way, grammar is to your paper what bricks and mortar are to a house's wall. One hopes neither sentences nor bricks will collapse as a result of sloppy construction.

Paragraph development is also a question of organized construction. If a word is a unit of thought, and if a sentence is one complete thought, then a paragraph is one complete thought expanded upon fully. Students who have had difficulty in the past with run-on sentences did so because they have placed two or more complete thoughts in one sentence. Similarly, students who have had difficulty with paragraph flow did so because they have forgotten that like a sentence, a paragraph is expected to house thoughts and examples related to only one idea. These students have, moreover, forgotten the paragraph's basic structure: topic sentence, body, and transition sentence. A topic sentence refers back to the paper's thesis while it suggests its paragraph's content. A transition sentence concludes the idea housed in its paragraph's body while it suggests the next paragraph's content. Your writing professor considers topic and transition sentences to be a paragraph's most important sentences because they keep a paper moving forward. Paragraph development, then, is akin to construction of a home's walls. Each paragraph, or wall, must be connected firmly to the next.

Citation of outside sources involves organization, too, but it is much more a matter of substantiation and ornamentation. A student has three reasons to cite work belonging to others: 1) citations give authors credit where credit is due; 2) citations link your paper to the works of established authors explicitly; and 3) citations make it easy for your readers to find the materials you have cited for themselves. What a student's citations look like is a far less interesting proposition since so little imagination is required, and citations are to conform exactly to a citation style. Although most academic departments have their own citation styles, two styles, American Psychological Association (APA) and Modern Language Association (MLA), are nevertheless employed by departments across the university. One could say APA and MLA have become the Celsius and Fahrenheit of the research world. What of Kelvin? Okay, we will describe *The Chicago Manual of Style* (CMS) as Kelvin. In any event, both APA and MLA call for citations to contain notably similar kinds of text-related information. It is ultimately the physical layout, the ornamentation, of the called-for textual information that differentiates the two citation styles. Yes, APA style is to be used in papers dealing with the social sciences, and MLA style is to be used in paper dealing with the arts and most humanities, but the ornamental differences between them are so slight the casual observer would scarcely notice difference in scholastic intent. Your professors, however, take their pet citation styles' appearances very seriously, and many students' papers have failed as a result of careless style application. Moving beyond substantiation and ornamentation, citation is one more thing to consider when you develop your paragraphs. You will recall citations are not to be placed just anywhere. Rather, quoted materials are to be placed where they will do the most good for your argument. Moreover, each citation is to be introduced by at least one sentence, and explained by at least one sentence. Only in the very rarest of circumstances will a citation start or end a paragraph. Citations, then, are like a building's decorative columns: they lend support, and look good doing so.

Review Of Grammar

The following review sheds light on incorrect and ineffective grammar usage found frequently in student writing. It is squarely the students' responsibility to apply this advice to their written work. One measure of intelligence is the ability to avoid past errors.

Adjectives and Adverbs

- Adjectives enhance nouns. Adverbs enhance adjectives, other adverbs, and verbs.

Correct: Debbie, a trifling student, talks quite scandalous**ly**.
Incorrect: Debbie, a trifling student, talks quite scandalous.

- Bad, good, near, real, and sure are adjectives. Badly, near, nearly, really, surely, and well are adverbs. Notice how many adverbs end with "ly".

Correct: Debbie did **well** on her exam.
Incorrect: Debbie did good on her exam.

- You are to avoid split infinitives by making sure adverbs follow verbs.

Correct: Debbie **scrambled** the eggs **briskly**.
Incorrect: Debbie briskly scrambled the eggs.

- Words performing as a single adjective or a "compound modifier" are to be hyphenated.

For example: two-lane highway, teriyaki-glazed onions, well-known dessert
Another example: Debbie ate **teriyaki-glazed** onions.

- However, no hyphenation is needed when a compound modifier is placed after a noun.

For example: Debbie's onions were **teriyaki glazed**.

- Hyphens are needed when compound numbers are spelled out.

For example: thirty-six, thirty-six years old

- Most prefixes require hyphens.

For example: anti-German, ex-boyfriend, mid-July, mid-1830s, pre-Second World War, self-assured, senator-elect, T-shirt

Agreement: Pronoun

- A pronoun is a word that can take the place of a noun. Some pronouns are:

he, him, his; I, me, mine; she, her, hers; they, them, theirs

- You are to make sure the pronouns match in kind and number.

Correct:	Students should bring **their** pencils.
Incorrect:	A student should bring their pencil.

Agreement: Subject and Verb

- A plural verb is called for when "and" joins a subject with multiple nouns or pronouns.

Correct:	Debbie **and** her cousins **are** at the club.
Incorrect:	Debbie and her cousins is at the club.

- A singular verb is needed if "or" or "nor" join multiple singular nouns or pronouns.

Correct	Either the lipstick case or the switchblade is in Debbie's purse.
Incorrect:	Either the lipstick case or the switchblade are in Debbie's purse.

- A verb is to agree with the subject, and not with a phrase's noun or pronoun.

Correct:	**Debbie**, as well as her cousins, **is** dancing.
Incorrect:	Debbie, as well as her cousins, are dancing.

- A verb is to agree with the portion of the subject nearest to it if "or" or "nor" join a singular and a plural noun or pronoun in a compound subject.

Correct:	Debbie or her **cousins dance** every night.
Incorrect:	Debbie or her cousins dances every night.

- Unless "I" or "you" is employed, "don't" is to be used only with a plural subject. "Doesn't," on the other hand, is to be employed only with a singular subject.

Correct: **Debbie doesn't** like small earrings.
Incorrect: Debbie don't like small earrings.

- The following words and phrases are singular and require singular verbs:

Anybody, anyone, each, each one, everybody, everyone, neither, nobody, no one, nobody, somebody, someone

Correct: **Each** of Debbie's cousins **dances** poorly.
Incorrect: Each of Debbie's cousins dance poorly.

- Singular nouns referring to more than one more person require a singular verb.

Correct: Debbie's **family has** a lot of drama.
Incorrect: Debbie's family have a lot of drama.

- The subject is to follow the verb when a sentence begins with "there is" or "there are"; however, because "there" is not the sentence's subject, the verb is to agree with what follows.

Correct: There **are** many **questions** in Debbie's mind.
Incorrect: There is many questions in Debbie's mind.

- Nonessential detail does not make a singular subject plural.

Correct: **Debbie**, accompanied by Pam, **is** traveling to Titusville.
Incorrect: Debbie, accompanied by Pam, are traveling to Titusville.

- Nouns describing items made of more than one part require plural verbs.

Correct: Debbie's **pants are** made of Lycra.
Incorrect: Debbie's pants is made of Lycra.

- However, some nouns ending with an "s" require singular verbs.

Correct: **"Rabies is** devastating," thought Debbie.
Incorrect: "Rabies are devastating," thought Debbie.

Article, Definite

- The definite article, an adjective, is written before a specific singular or plural noun.

For example: **The** car that struck Debbie sped away.

Articles, Indefinite

- Indefinite articles are also adjectives, but they are written before a general singular or plural noun.

For example: **A** cat jumped on Debbie's lap.

- "A" is used before most words that begin with consonants.

Correct: Debbie bought **a silver** lighter.
Incorrect: Debbie bought an silver lighter.

- However, "an" is used before words starting with an unsounded h.

Correct: Debbie made **an honest** mistake.

Incorrect: Debbie made a honest mistake.

- "An" is also used before most words that begin with vowels.

Correct: Debbie would have otherwise bought **an alligator** skin purse.
Incorrect: Debbie would have otherwise bought a alligator skin purse.

- Nevertheless, "a" is used if a "u" sounds like "y," or "o" sounds like "w."

Correct: Debbie's boyfriend, **a one-legged** man, gave Pam his phone number on **a used** napkin.
Incorrect: Debbie's boyfriend, an one-legged man, gave Pam his phone number on an used napkin.

- Indefinite articles cannot be used with noncount nouns.

Correct: Debbie spilled **the milk** on the floor accidentally.
Incorrect: Debbie spilled a milk on the floor accidentally.

Capitalization

- Academic degrees are made lowercase when they are written fully:

baccalaureate degree, bachelor's degree, bachelor of arts, bachelor of science, bachelor's degrees, master's degree, master of arts, master of science, master's degrees, doctoral degree doctorate, doctor of philosophy, doctoral degrees

- Academic degrees are abbreviated with periods:

B.A, B.S., B.A.'s, M.A., M.S., M.A.'s, M.S.'s, D.Ed., D.Ed.'s, M.D., M.D.'s, Ph.D., Ph.D.'s

- Names of majors, minors, and programs are lowercase, except for names pertaining to specific languages (e.g. English, German).

- For unit names, capitalize the first reference and lower case the second.

For example: Department of Rhetoric, the department; College of Writing, the college; Baron-Forness Library, the library; McComb Fieldhouse, the fieldhouse

The exception: Edinboro University of Pennsylvania; the University

- Other academic and seasonal terms include:

fall semester, spring semester, summer session, Fall 2007 semester, freshman, sophomore, junior, senior, spring, summer, fall, winter

- For position titles, use the lowercase except when preceding a name or when used in a mailing address.

For example: President Luca Brasi; Luca Brasi, president of Edinboro University of Pennsylvania; Assistant Professor Iona Trailer; Iona Trailer, assistant professor of sociology; the assistant professor

- Lowercase "e-mail" and "fax" in text; uppercase when either precede the number.

For example: send e-mail to itrailer@ediboro.edu; E-mail: itrailer@edinboro.edu; 814-867-5306 is the fax number; Fax: 814-867-5309

- Uppercase "Internet" and "Web" (when referring to the Internet) in text.

- Proper names of regions are to be capitalized, but general directions are to be lowercased.

For example: The Northwest, The West Coast, West Texas, eastern, northwestern Pennsylvania, ten miles south of here

- When used as proper names, titles belonging to family members are to be capitalized.

For example: Debbie gave candy to her Cousin Pookie, but not to her other cousins.
Here is a card I bought for Dad.
Did you help your father with the yard work?

- Capitalize the names of Gods, religious leaders, and holy books, but do not capitalize non-specific use of the word "god."

For example: God the father, Adoni, Saul, Hecate, the Comanche gods, the Torah, the Talmud, the Koran, the Bible, the Virgin Mary

- Capitalize the proper names of ethnic groups, but lowercase vernacular names of ethnic groups.

For example: African American, black, Caucasian, white

- Capitalize time periods and important occurrences, but not centuries.

For example: Elizabethan England, Little Ice Age, sixteenth century

Clauses: Dependent, Independent, Introductory, and Subordinate

- The most common example of an incomplete sentence, a dependent clause, has a subject and a verb, but does not represent a complete thought on its own.

For example: When Debbie dyed her hair sea foam green.
Correction: **When** Debbie dyed her hair sea foam green, **gentlemen showed interest in her**.

- A dependent marker word signifies a dependent clause. Some dependant marker words and phrases are:

after, although, as, as if, because, before, even if, even though, if, in order to, since, though, unless, until, when, whenever, whether, while

Note: A sentence beginning with any of the words or phrases listed above will contain a comma.

- A coordinating conjunction or connecting word is used to join a dependent and an independent clause. Coordinating conjunctions may also be used to join two independent clauses. If a sentence's second independent clause begins with a coordinating conjunction, place a comma before it. Some coordinating conjunctions are:

and, but, for, nor, or, so, yet

For example: Debbie dyed her hair sea foam green, **but** doing so failed to gain her Pam's affection.

- Another connecting word, the independent marker word, joins sentences that can stand alone. If a sentence's second independent clause begins with an independent marker word, place a semicolon before it. An independent marker word is usually followed by a comma. Some coordinating conjunctions are:

also, consequently, furthermore, however, moreover, nevertheless, rather, therefore

For example: Debbie's sea foam green hair had attracted the attention of gentlemen; **however,** she remained miserable as Pam had yet to give her the attention she had craved.

- An independent clause or sentence contains a subject and a verb and represents a complete thought.

For example: Debbie thought of attending Toni & Guy Hairdressing Academy.

- An introductory clause, which by itself is a dependent clause, establishes the context for an independent clause. Not surprisingly, introductory clauses employ dependant marker words.

For example: **If she wants to win Pam's affection,** Debbie will have to do something with her hair.

- Another name for a dependent clause, the subordinate clause, will create confusion if it interrupts the independent clause.

Correct: Future job opportunities **are lacking because** of Aladdin Beauty School's closure.
Incorrect: Future job opportunities, because of Aladdin Beauty School's closure, are lacking.

Commas

- A comma links dependent and independent clauses. A comma can also link two independent clauses, but only when a coordinating conjunction is placed between them.

Correct: Debbie went home quickly, **and** she intended to stay there.

Incorrect: Debbie went home quickly, she intended to stay there.

- Most introductory words and phrases are to be followed with commas.

For example: **Meanwhile,** Debbie sat in the closet nearest to her phone stand as she waited for Pam to call.

- Do not use a comma to separate subject from predicate.

Correct: Giving her apology to Pam for evaluation and possible publication **was** one of the most difficult tasks Debbie had ever attempted.

Incorrect: Giving her apology to Pam for evaluation and possible publication, was one of the most difficult tasks Debbie had ever attempted.

Commas and Nonessential Elements

- Use commas to separate nonessential clauses, phrases, and words from a sentence.

Correct: Debbie, **who is 5'5" tall,** found work at the local coffee shop.

Incorrect: Debbie who is 5'5" tall found work at the local coffee shop.

Comma Splices

A comma splice occurs when a comma is placed between two independent clauses.

Correct: Debbie disliked her work at the coffee shop. It was very demeaning.
Incorrect: Debbie disliked her work at the coffee shop, it was very demeaning.

Dangling Modifiers

A dangling modifier explains or illustrates a word or phrase not stated clearly in a sentence.

Correct: **Debbie failed** her experiment, not having studied human nature carefully.
Incorrect: The experiment was a failure, not having studied human nature carefully.

Fused Sentences

- Like a run-on, a fused sentence occurs when no connecting word or punctuation separates two independent clauses.

Correct: Debbie stole Baron-Forness Library's only copy of *The Story of O*. Each librarian now considers her a sneak thief.
Incorrect: Debbie stole Baron-Forness Library's only copy of *The Story of O* each librarian now considers her a sneak thief.

Run-on Sentences

- A run-on occurs when no connecting word or punctuation separates two independent clauses.

Correct: Debbie was not misunderstood; the others knew she was a thief.
Incorrect: Debbie was not misunderstood the others knew she was a thief.

Semicolons

- Semicolons link two independent clauses without connecting words.

For example: Pam did not see herself as Debbie's artistic muse; she posed because she needed the money.

Sentence Fragments

- A sentence fragment occurs when an incomplete thought is taken to be a complete sentence.

Correct: Because Debbie confused the state of being misunderstood with the state of being an artist, **she went about speaking incoherently.**

Incorrect: Because Debbie confused the state of being misunderstood with the state of being an artist.

Sentence Types

- Simple Sentence

Characteristics: Independent clause [.]

For example: Debbie was concerned about the evolution of German feminism.

- Compound Sentence A

Characteristics: Independent clause [,] coordinating conjunction independent clause [.]

For example: Debbie was concerned about the evolution of German feminism, **but** she did not know exactly why.

- Compound Sentence B

Characteristics: Independent clause [;] independent clause [.]

For example: Debbie was concerned about the evolution of German feminism; she was unsure of the nature of her interest.

- Compound Sentence C

Characteristics: Independent clause [;] independent marker [,] independent clause [.]

For example: Debbie was concerned about the evolution of German feminism; **therefore,** she decided to visit Berlin.

- Complex Sentence A

Characteristics: Dependent marker dependent clause [,] independent clause [.]

For example: **Because** Debbie was concerned about the evolution of German feminism, she decided to visit Berlin.

- Complex Sentence B

Characteristics: Independent clause dependent marker dependent clause [.]

For example: Debbie was concerned about the evolution of German feminism **because** it was fashionable in some groups to be so.

- Complex Sentence C

Characteristics: First part of an independent clause [,] nonessential clause or phrase [,] rest of the independent clause [.]

For example: Many young women, **including Debbie and her cousins,** were concerned about the evolution of German feminism.

- Complex Sentence D

Characteristics: First part of an independent clause essential clause or phrase rest of the independent clause [.]

For example: Many young women **who were concerned about the evolution of German feminism** decided to visit Berlin.

Time and Numbers

- Days and years can be expressed as follows:

April 23, 1971; 23 April 1971; in 1971; the seventies; the 1970s (APA); the 1970's

- There are a number of ways to record time of day:

7:55 A.M., 7:55 P.M., 7:55 a.m., 7:55 p.m., six o'clock in the morning, 11 o'clock at night, half-past five in the afternoon, 15 minutes to 3 p.m.

- Use numerals to express numbers 10 and above, and use words to express numbers below 10.

For example: Debbie did not mind wearing clear plastic heels that made her appear **five**-inches taller than she was.

- Use numerals to express all numbers when you are discussing more than one number in the same sentence.

For example: Of the **12** gentlemen interested in Debbie, **4** were eliminated from her cell phone's contact list by the second week of her social experiment.

- Figures may take on the following appearances:

5%, after 30 days, only $19.95, a 1.35 GPA, five percent, $4 billion, 2.5 gallons, two five-question tests

- Addresses are written like this:

10 Tenth Street, 2016 West 42 Street

- Use numerals to express identification numbers, like so:

Channel 200, chapter 6, Henry IV, Interstate 79, page 10, Room 5

- Numbers in series and statistics need to be consistent.

For example: two turntables and one microphone, 10 feet by 20 feet, 10' x 20', 30 to 6, 30-6

- Do not begin a sentence with a number.

Correct: **Giant** Eagle sold 12 dozen apples today.
Incorrect: 12 dozen apples were sold at Giant Eagle today.

The Pennsylvania Exception

- The phrase, "to be" is not to be excluded from a sentence unnecessarily.

| Correct: | Debbie's lawn needs **to be** mowed. |
| Incorrect: | Debbie's lawn needs mowed. |

Vagueness

- Avoid forming ambiguous sentences.

| Correct: | Although Debbie's **bicycle** hit the tree, the **bicycle** was not damaged. |
| Incorrect: | Although Debbie's bicycle hit the tree, there was no damage. |

- An active-voice sentence points out a verb's doer(s).

| Correct: | **Debbie and her cousins** decided to go to the club. |
| Incorrect: | A decision was made to go to the club. |

- Avoid turning noun into verbs.

| Correct: | The women's decision **was applied** immediately. |
| Incorrect: | The application of the women's decision was immediate. |

Verb Tenses

- Six basic verb tenses allow students to reflect time in their writing. The six tenses are:

Simple Present

For example: Debbie **walks** to Pam's trailer.

Present Perfect

For example: Debbie **has walked** to Pam's trailer.

Simple Past

For example: Debbie **walked to** Pam's trailer.

Past Perfect

For example: Debbie **had walked** to Pam's trailer.

Future

For example: Debbie **will walk** to Pam's trailer.

Future Perfect

For example: Debbie **will have** walked to Pam's trailer.

I am going to let you in on a little secret: if you come from an English-speaking home, you know much more about English grammar than you think you do. You have practiced this grammar from the moment you began to speak, and you have communicated more and more successfully with your friends and family ever since. As a thinking individual, you have acquired vocabulary every year; even more so if you have made it a point to read books for fun. If you have had the benefit of caring teachers in grade school who demonstrated their concern for your academic progress by correcting your grammar often, you have learned therc is indeed a difference between formal and informal speaking and writing. In short, while you may not yet be able to name grammar rules, chances are you know what sounds right and what does not. Moreover, there is absolutely no reason for you to consider yourself a blathering idiot like so many students do when the subject of grammar comes up in class. You enter your Freshman Composition classroom with enough know-how to write papers with a minimum of grammatical errors. For you, all that may be left in regard to grammar is to enforce a strict sense of self-discipline that will prohibit you from making the same errors found in your high school writing. Truly, your writing professor prefers you to make new grammatical mistakes than repeat the old.

Nevertheless, what about those students for whom English is a second language? Or those other students, for whom reading was not encouraged at home, and consequently possess a smaller vocabulary than life-long readers? Or yet further students, who did not benefit from the grammatical corrections offered by caring grade school teachers? To them I say, do not give up hope. The vast majority of people taking Freshman Composition are just beginning their higher education; they will have at least four years to get their use of grammar up to a professional level. No one is born a writer, and the sooner one imitates choices made by professional writers', the sooner one's grammar level will catch-up with that of one's more privileged classmates. Following the advice below will begin this important process.

1.   Do not write like you speak. Speaking is more of an informal, spontaneous affair than writing is. While one is often free to speak off the cuff during a fast-paced, personal conversation, people give writing a far greater level of scrutiny because it takes time; writing is a careful, unhurried, objective expression of one's thoughts. Your spoken grammatical mistakes can get lost easily within a conversation, but people will judge your writing for as long as the paper it is printed on exists.

2.   Separate yourself momentarily from the dialect you use among friends and family. Dialects are cultural or local forms of a mother language. In a way, dialects help identify one group of people from another, and when you employ a dialect, you are showing membership with your group almost to the exclusion of other groups. Problems related to understanding arise when your dialect's grammar is markedly different from grammar belonging to formal writing. For example, I grew up in western New York. When I was a young child, my grandfather once told me, "Is you deef? I told you to get them cranes away from the crick or we'll wrassle." I knew my grandfather was not tell-

ing me to move my tall, white birds away from the muscle
spasm; rather, in our shared western New York dialect he
was warning me to move my *crayons* away from the *creek*
("deef" and "wrassle" were how members of his generation
of western New Yorkers pronounced *deaf* and *wrestle*).

3.   Do not take the easy way out. Contractions (e.g. can't for
cannot, doesn't for does not, isn't for is not) are viewed by
writing professors as too informal for college-level work.
It is better that you invest the few extra seconds and type
words completely. Much worse, however, is allowing Text
Speak (e.g. b/c, gr8, ur) to ooze into your writing. Nothing will make you appear more like a 13-year old punk kid
waiting at the mall for a ride home than having typed your
paper like you would a text message. Lastly, when spelling, depend on your dictionary more than sounding words
out. Writing professors are hard on misspelling because
the problem is an easy fix.

4.   Make reading your first priority. Yes, do your assigned
nightly reading, but also be sure to read for pleasure. Read
anything you can get your hands on, and then read some
more. When it comes right down to it, and in regard to
grammar skill, what really separates advanced, beginning,
and functionally illiterate student writers is the amount of
time they have spent reading. Just as imitating the moves
of favorite athletes is much easier to do if the amateur invests a great deal of time in studying and practicing the
athletes' work, the student who takes active note of how
his or her favorite published authors have used grammar
has a large grammar playbook to refer to. The neat thing
is you need not have been a star student in grade school to
improve your grammar now. You will be surprised by the
speed with which your brain responds to mental exercise.
I have frequently seen nontraditional students who gradu-
ated high school 10 or 20 years ago outscore students who
are recent high school graduates.

Paragraph Development

Paragraph development is all about strategy; it is simply a matter of knowing what you will write and where you will write it for the greatest persuasive effect. The best tool for paragraph development is the outline. Like professional writers, you will actually dedicate more time to paragraph development than you will to writing. Doing so has five advantages. First, paragraph development removes almost all of the guesswork from the writing of your paper, and thus, you save a great deal of time while at your computer. Next, paragraph development keeps your argument on track because your outline will show you your argument's established progression; you are much less likely to stray from a path you created. Further, paragraph development shows you where your argument is in most need of outside support. When you know precisely where quoted materials will do the most good for your argument, you will no longer throw in quotes merely because a teacher asked for them (to this end, never ask your writing professor, "How many quotes do I need?"). Also, paragraph development allows you to place emotion into your work tactically. You will know exactly when to move your public to feel what you want it to feel. Further still, paragraph development removes the clutter from your workplace, because bringing a typed outline with you to your computer is a far less burdensome task than carrying and organizing a stack of books, journal articles, and notes.

Paragraph development requires complete dedication to your written project. Notice how my discussion of paragraph development's advantages above made no suggestion of writing a paper the night before it is due. On the contrary, a writing professor can sniff-out poorly planned, hasty writing quickly; like a nervous skunk under a porch, the procrastinator's work sprays its own kind of unmistakable stink. No, you will not be among those students who procrastinate because you know the stakes are too high for that silliness. That said, let us review.

Earlier in this chapter, I told you a word is a unit of thought, a sentence is one complete thought, and a paragraph is one complete thought expanded upon fully. A paragraph has no set length;

a paragraph can be two sentences long, a page long, or any length in between. Because a paragraph's length is determined solely by the needs of the thought you are expressing, you can forget what your high school English teacher may have said about a paragraph having to be 3 to 5 sentences in length. More complex ideas will require more room to grow than less complex ideas. A body paragraph, however, has two constants: a topic sentence and a transition sentence. Again, a topic sentence refers back to the paper's thesis while it suggests its paragraph's content. A transition sentence, on the other hand, concludes the idea housed in its paragraph's body while it suggests the next paragraph's content. Living between a paragraph's topic and transition sentences are its body sentences. Body sentences are interesting because they contain information belonging to three levels of importance: primary, secondary, and tertiary. You will place your best (primary) examples and ideas closest to a paragraph's topic sentence because you want your public to read them first. Conversely, you will place your minor (tertiary) examples and ideas just before a paragraph's transition sentence. That way, if paper length requirements call on you to remove less important text, you can do so easily from the bottom up. For example:

A. Topic sentence
    1. Primary examples and ideas
    2. Secondary examples and ideas
    3. Tertiary examples and ideas
B. Transition sentence

It will help you to imagine body paragraphs as Lego construction bricks. Each paragraph, or piece, is to fit together seamlessly, as in:

A. Topic sentence
    1. Primary examples and ideas
    2. Secondary examples and ideas
    3. Tertiary examples and ideas
B. Transition sentence

C.   Topic sentence
    1.   Primary examples and ideas
    2.   Secondary examples and ideas
    3.   Tertiary examples and ideas
D.   Transition sentence

Making room for quoted materials within a body paragraph is no problem, either. Just remember each quotation is to be introduced by at least one sentence, and explained by at least one sentence. For instance:

A.   Topic sentence
    1.   Primary examples and ideas
    2.   Secondary examples and ideas
        a.   Introduction to quotation
        b.   Quotation
        c.   Explanation of quotation
    3.   Tertiary examples and ideas
B.   Transition sentence

The choice to introduce, place, and explain the quotation under "Secondary examples and ideas" is deliberate. For one, the space given to "Primary examples and ideas" is reserved for your thoughts alone. After reading the paragraph's topic sentence, your public moves on to this important space, and you want to make sure its attention is directed first on your ideas. Incorporating a quotation there would suggest to your public, "Hey, listen to what this other guy has to say. I'll just wait in the background." Nor do you want to incorporate a quotation in the space given to "Tertiary examples and ideas". Minor examples and ideas go there. If you consider a particular quotation to be of only minor importance, it is better to leave it out. Remember, quoted materials should make up no more than ten percent of any paper. Again, quotations lend support to a point you are making; quotations do not make your point for you.

At this point you likely find yourself saying, "Okay, he has talked about body paragraphs. I thought you start an essay with an introductory paragraph?" This question is not without merit. An introductory paragraph does, in fact, begin an essay, but you may be surprised to learn most professional writers actually plan their introductory paragraphs *after* they have developed their body paragraphs. The reason is simple: it is much easier to introduce something that exists. Planning an introductory paragraph before you develop your body paragraphs leaves too much work for your imagination. More specifically, doing so forces you to plan an introductory paragraph based almost purely on supposition; you suppose the paper you are introducing will consist of this or that. On the other hand, knowing exactly what your paper consists of prior to planning your introductory paragraph makes for one of the easiest tasks. When you look at the introductory paragraph outline below, think back to your introduction to Inventio in Chapter 1. Notice how much your body paragraphs feed your introductory paragraph's content:

A. Topic sentence
    1. Ideas related to the need for your argument
    2. Ideas related to the significance of your argument
    3. Ideas related to the history of your argument
    4. Ideas related to the terms most important to your argument
    5. Ideas related to the prejudice you bring to your argument
B. Thesis statement

I mentioned earlier that every flaw in research belonging to others is an open window of opportunity for you. I further suggested you may take full advantage of these flaws, and show your work to be a solution to them, if you dedicate significant space within the body of your paper to establishing the need for your argument, as well as to speaking to your argument's significance and history. It should come as no shock, then, when mention of these endeavors is to figure so prominently in your introductory paragraph. The same goes for making your introductory paragraph home to discussion of terms most important to your argument and mention of the prejudice you bring to your argument. Just as you want to reinforce the idea you know what you are talking about as soon as possible, you want your intentions to appear aboveboard from the start.

Developing a concluding paragraph is an even easier task. As long as you avoid the common beginning writer mistake of attempting to rewrite your paper in your concluding paragraph, this bit will be fairly brief (you will also avoid the redundant phrase, "In conclusion" here; your public is bright enough to notice there are no paragraphs following). A concluding
paragraph has five components:

A. Rewarded thesis statement
   1. Restating of paper's goals
   2. Description of paper's findings
   3. Description of paper's limitations
   4. Description of paper's implications on future research in the same subject area

Notice how concluding takes on a specific meaning. While concluding can mean ending, conclusion can mean last portion, and concluding as it is used here refers to deciding, as in, "She concluded she likes fried clams." Thus, a concluding paragraph is a space reserved for final verdicts. You will find your writing professor has this latter definition in mind when he or she speaks of the definite need to resolve one's argument.

Just as paragraphs do not have set lengths, most essays do not have a set number of paragraphs. In the main, an essay can have as many paragraphs as its author has thoughts; after all, a paragraph constitutes only one complete thought. The exception to this freedom is found in paper length requirements defined by your writing professor. That most elementary paper, the five-paragraph essay, comes to mind. While I am loathe to assign my students the five-paragraph essay, a project I consider far more appropriate for the high school English classroom, looking at the outline of such a basic structure will nevertheless prove useful. For example:

A.   Topic sentence
    1.   Ideas related to the need for your argument
    2.   Ideas related to the significance of your argument
    3.   Ideas related to the history of your argument
    4.   Ideas related to the terms most important to your argument
    5.   Ideas related to the prejudice you bring to your argument
B.   Thesis statement
C.   Topic sentence
    1.   Primary examples and ideas
    2.   Secondary examples and ideas
    3.   Tertiary examples and ideas
D.   Transition sentence
E.   Topic sentence
    1.   Primary examples and ideas
    2.   Secondary examples and ideas
    3.   Tertiary examples and ideas
F.   Transition sentence
G.   Topic sentence
    1.   Primary examples and ideas
    2.   Secondary examples and ideas
    3.   Tertiary examples and ideas
H.   Transition sentence
I.   Reworded thesis statement
    1.   Restating of paper's goals
    2.   Description of paper's findings
    3.   Description of paper's limitations
    4.   Description of paper's implications on future research in the same subject area

The outline above reminds one of a bare skeleton in need of muscles, ligaments, and tendons. Now, exactly how does one go about making this fellow ambulatory? You will start your paragraph development by paying strict attention to the very basics. The 10 steps below will assist you greatly in creating an outline and filling in its blanks. First, however, an important reminder is in order: your paragraph development cannot begin until you have decided upon a thesis. Again, a thesis is an essential, precise, guiding argument that will be defended in *each* of your paper's paragraphs. Be sure to revisit my discussions of stasis, thesis, and counter-thesis in Chapter 1 as often as you need to.

1. Decide how many ideas you have in regard to your argument, and list them from most important to least. This amount will become the approximate number of body paragraphs your essay will have (Do not worry, you are free to add or subtract body paragraphs as you revise).

2. Construct your body paragraph outline, making sure you have one body paragraph template for each of your ideas (see examples above).

3. Compose a topic sentence for each of your body paragraphs, and place them on your outline. You will recall a topic sentence refers back to the paper's thesis while it suggests its paragraph's content.

4. Make sure you have listed your body paragraphs in the order of most important idea to least.

5. Compose a transition sentence for each of your body paragraphs, and place them on your outline. Remember, a transition sentence concludes the idea housed in its paragraph's body while it suggests the next paragraph's content.

6. Come up with ideal examples and ideas for each point your topic sentences make, and list them next to "Primary examples and ideas." These will emphasize your originality in thinking.

7. Conduct research, and find one or two quotes that will support each point your topic sentences make. You will not, of course, use all of these gathered quotes, but having an array of back up to choose from is important.

8. Choose the fewest quotes you believe are most important to your paper, and incorporate them into your paragraphs in need of the most outside support. List them next to Sec-

ondary examples and ideas." Do not forget to sandwich each quote with introductory and explanatory sentences.

9. Come up with minor examples and ideas for each point your topic sentences make, and list them next to "Tertiary examples and ideas." Like salt on a steak, these minor examples and ideas will lend flavor to your paragraphs.

10. Conduct revision, making sure each of your topic sentences refer back to your thesis. Also make sure all primary, secondary, and tertiary examples refer back to their topic sentences. Check your flow by making sure each body paragraph's transition sentence concludes the idea housed in its body while it suggests the next paragraph's content. Ask yourself if your quotes have been placed strategically. Note if each quote has been introduced by at least one sentence, and explained by at least one sentence.

You may develop your introductory and concluding paragraphs once you have finished outlining your body paragraphs.

A meaty outline makes for easy essay writing. The more thorough you make your outline, the less you will struggle at your computer, hoping desperately another idea, sentence, or word will come to you. Make no mistake; developing your paragraphs will take no small amount of time. But doing so is time very well spent. Such planning is the hallmark of a professional writer. That said, there is just one more paragraph-related mission you must accomplish: you are now to plan exactly when to move your public to feel the emotions that you want it to feel.

I have suggested earlier that incorporating emotions into your essay is a persuasive move meant to arouse noticeable feelings among your public. An emotional public is disarmed; if you are able to capture your public's heart, you will soon capture your public's head. To this end, your sad tale is triumphant only if you get your public to reach for Kleenex. Likewise, your comedic tale is triumphant only if you make your public chuckle. You thus play the puppet master when you write an essay. Answering the four questions below will help you to pull your public's heartstrings. Place your answers to these pathos-themed questions parallel to your essay's outline.

1.   What mood do I wish to set for my public in my introductory paragraph?
     a.   What words and phrases lend the most to this mood?
     b.   What words and phrases lend the least to this mood?
2.   Where in my essay is it most appropriate to reinforce this mood?
     a.   Exactly where should I place my set-ups?
     b.   Exactly where should I place my punch lines or climactic phrases?
3.   Where in my essay is it most appropriate to let up on this mood?
     a.   Exactly where should I give my audience breathers?
     b.   Exactly where will these breathers actually strengthen my next punch line or climactic phrase?
4.   What mood do I want to leave my public with in my concluding paragraph?
     a.   Is this final mood more likely to assist me in persuading my public to follow my call to action?
     b.   Is this final mood a feeling my public can appreciate?

Some of these questions call to mind well-known, pathos-based strategies. The notion of the breather, for instance, is common to horror movies. A horror movie director will allow his or her audience to relax a bit after a scare in order make the next scare more startling; the architectural layouts of haunted houses and funhouses run on the same principle. Commercials, especially those involving charities, will often set one mood, but will end with another, as the American audience tends to appreciate a sense of hope, a happy ending. For example, "This little girl has no shoes for her feet, and she will go to bed hungry again tonight. For only 10 dollars a month, thanks to you, little Han Mulan can have a much better life."

Introduction to Citation

APA Style

"APA," a pet name given to the strictly enforced citation rules set forth by the American Psychological Association, is used within the social sciences (e.g. anthropology, psychology, sociology). That is to say, if your major is centered on the study of people, or if the paper you are writing deals with the study of people, APA is the style you will need to use.

APA In-text Citation

"In-text citation" refers simply to citing or documenting materials you have quoted and placed within the paper you are writing. In this regard, APA style gives you a few options to consider.

Option 1, Print Source

(Author's last name, year of publication, page number)

For example: "She turned from him evidently much shocked or offended, but presently recovered her composure and told him gently that a leg was never mentioned before ladies: the proper word was limb" (Mencken, 1970, p. 302).

Note: Notice how the citation is sandwiched between the quotation mark and the period, which I will refer to later as terminal punctuation.

Option 2, Print Source

Author's last name—(year of publication)—transition phrase—"quote"—(page number)

For example: Mencken (1970) tells us, "Even chickens ceased to have legs" (p. 302).

Option 3, Print Source, Quote-within-a-quote

(Quoted author's last name, year of his or her publication, as cited in quoting author's last name, publication date, page number)

For example: "Even chickens ceased to have legs, and another British traveler, W.F. Goodmane, was 'not a little confused on being requested by a lady, at a public dinner table, to furnish her with the first and second joint'" (Goodmane, 1845, as cited in Mencken, 1970, p. 302).

Note: Notice how single quotation marks separate Goodmane's quote from Mencken's.

Option 4, Print Source, Block Quote (a quote of 40 or more words)

Author's last name—(year of publication)—transition phrase—colon -quote without quotation marks—each line indented five spaces from left margin—terminal punctuation—(page number)

For example: Sideris (2007) has suggested to his staff:

Many students today mistakenly assume the gaining of an ability to write well is similar to the buying of a super-sized value meal at the local fast food drive-through. All they need to do is pull up, pay, sit quietly until something substantial is handed to them (be it burgers and fries or, in the case of writing classes, passing grades), and once the sale is completed, leave quickly. Although few of these students would purchase a super-sized value meal as a remedy for life-long poor nutrition, many students will come to class believing a short term investment in one or two writing courses will somehow cure years of piece-meal reading and writing practice. (p. 55)

Option 5, Print Source, Holy Book

(Abbreviated book name. Chapter: Verse: *Holy book's version name italicized*)

For example: "There she lusted after her lovers, whose flesh was like that of donkeys and whose emission was like that of stallions" (Ezek. 23:20: *New International Version*).

Note: You do not need to identify the version in subsequent references unless you switch to a different version.

Another note: According to the APA Publication Manual (2001), reference entries are not needed for the Bible and other major classical works. However, your professor may require full publication information. If you are not sure, ask him or her.

Option 6, Web Source

(Author's last name or site's sponsor's name, year of publication or of uploading, paragraph symbol paragraph number)

For example: "The Hebrew prophets frequently compared the sin of idolatry to the sin of adultery, in a frequently reappearing rhetorical figure" (Wikipedia contributors, 2007, ¶ 3).

Option 7, Web Source

Author's last name or site's sponsor's name—(year of publication or of uploading)—transition phrase—"quote"—(paragraph symbol paragraph number)

For example: Wikipedia's contributors (2007) suggest "The Hebrew prophets frequently compared the sin of idolatry to the sin of adultery, in a frequently reappearing rhetorical figure" (¶ 3).

APA and Paraphrasing

To paraphrase is to restate a passage in *your own* words while keeping the author's ideas intact. In other words, it is to summarize an idea rather than quote it directly.

Author's last name (year of publication) summary

For example: Vonnegut (1966) speaks of human life as being cheap.

APA and the Interview

APA does not consider interviews to be recoverable data, so they will not be placed on a references page. However, you are to cite them in your text, like so:

Interviewee's first initial Intervicwee's last name (personal communication, Month day, year) interviewee's statement

For example: J. Sideris (personal communication, July 9, 2007) indicated "the student was quite insane, to the point of boorishness."

Symbols Common to APA and their Application

p. (page, as in p. 5), pp. (pages, as in pp. 5-10), ¶ (paragraph, as in ¶ 3)

Note: A space has to be placed between the symbol and its number(s).

Another Note: You may find the paragraph symbol on Word by going to Insert to Symbol to More Symbols to Latin 1.

APA Bibliographical Citation

A bibliography is an *alphabetical* list of citations to books, articles, and other documents found at the end of your paper. An APA bibliography is called References. On it, you will list only what you have used in your paper.

Book, Single Author

Baxter, C. (1997). *Race equality in health care and education.* New York: Penguin.

Book, Two Authors

Smith, G., & Johnson, T. (2000). *Your failure to please others.* New York: Harcourt.

Book, Three or More Authors

Kernis, M. H., Cornell, D. P., & Sun, C. R. (1993). *Emo: Pure pretension.* London: Apple.

Chapter in a Book

Jones, T. (1995). Teen angst. In J. Holmes & D. Diggler (Eds.), *Textbook of the misunderstood* (pp. 69-72). Baltimore: Nova.

Dictionary

Doe, J. (Ed.). (1980). *The dictionary of American music.* (2nd ed.). London: Penguin.

Encyclopedia Entry

Rourke, H. (1993). Egoism. In *The new Ayn Rand encyclopedia*. New York: Francon Press.

Journal Article

Bowles, A. (1966). The psychology of the spy. *British Journal of Psychiatry, 141,* 171-177.

Note: The italicized number is the journal's volume number.

Another Note: Journal articles are referred to as articles, not as "entries." Diaries have entries.

Magazine Article

Benz, M. (2007, July 9). Paris Hilton: The appeal of mindlessness. *New Yorker*, 36-41.

Newspaper Article

Benz, M. (2007, July 9). Paris Hilton: The appeal of mindlessness. *The Washington Post*, p. C12.

Note: Should no author be listed, flip title before date and alphabetize citation accordingly.

Government Document / Pamphlet

Center for Disease Control. (1996). *Syphilis is not an appropriate Valentine's Day gift*. (CDC Publication No. 12-3456). Atlanta: U.S. Government Printing Office.

Electronic Version of a Print Source

Knowles, B. (2007). How to get him to sweat-out your flip. [Electronic Version]. *Urban Inquiry, 25,* 590-625.

A Webpage Without an Author

Better pickling methods. (2006). Retrieved from the Web July 9, 2007. http://www.recipes.com

A Webpage With an Author

Stewart, M. (2006). Better pickling methods. Retrieved from the Web July 9, 2007. http://www.recipes.com

Film

Smith, K. (Producer), & Reed, R. (Director). (2009). *Hip new teen movie* [Motion picture]. United States: Paramount Pictures.

Television Series

Davis, D. (Producer). (2007). *Average sitcom* [Television series]. Hollywood: American Broadcasting Company.

Song

Bruce, K. (1992). Kiss him for me. On *Your man is my man* [CD]. New York: Polygram Music.

MLA Style

"MLA," a nickname given to the citation rules set forth by the Modern Language Association, is used within the humanities (e.g. art, English, music). That is to say, if your major is centered on the study of human creativity, or if the paper you are writing deals with the study of human creativity, MLA is the style you will need to use.

MLA In-text Citation

"In-text citation" refers simply to documenting or citing materials you have quoted and placed within the paper you are writing. In this regard, MLA style gives you a few options to consider.

Option 1, Print Source

(Author's last name page number)

For example: "She turned from him evidently much shocked or offended, but presently recovered her composure and told him gently that a leg was never mentioned before ladies: the proper word was limb" (Mencken 302).

Note: Notice how the citation is sandwiched between the quotation mark and the period, which I have referred to earlier as terminal punctuation.

Option 2, Print Source

Author's last name—transition phrase—"quote"—(page number)

For example: Mencken tells us, "Even chickens ceased to have legs" (302).

Option 3, Print Source, Quote-within-a-quote
(Quoted author's last name qtd. in quoting author's last name page number)

For example: "Even chickens ceased to have legs, and another British traveler, W.F. Goodmane, was 'not a little confused on being requested by a lady, at a public dinner table, to furnish her with the first and second joint'" (Goodmane qtd. in Mencken 302).

Note: Notice how single quotation marks separate Goodmane's work from Mencken's.

Option 4, Print Source, Block Quote (a quote of 4 or more lines)

Introductory or transition phrase—colon -quote without quotation marks—each line indented ten spaces from left margin—terminal punctuation—(author's last name page number)

For example: The subject of student laziness is a common one among professors because:

Many students today mistakenly assume the gaining of an ability to write well is similar to the buying of a super-sized value meal at the local fast food drive-through. All they need to do is pull up, pay, sit quietly until something substantial is handed to them (be it burgers and fries or, in the case of writing classes, passing grades), and once the sale is completed, leave quickly. Although few of these students would purchase a super-sized value meal as a remedy for life-long poor nutrition, many students will come to class believing a short term investment in one or two writing courses will somehow cure years of piece-meal reading and writing practice. (Sideris 55)

Option 5, Print Source, Holy Book

(*Holy book's version name italicized*, Abbreviated book name. Chapter. Verse)

For example: "There she lusted after her lovers, whose flesh was like that of donkeys and whose emission was like that of stallions" (*New International Version*, Ezek. 23.20).

Note: You do not need to identify the version in subsequent references unless you switch to a different version.

Option 6, Web Source

(Website's name paragraph symbol paragraph number)

For example: "The Hebrew prophets frequently compared the sin of idolatry to the sin of adultery, in a frequently reappearing rhetorical figure" (Wikipedia ¶ 3).

Option 7, Web Source

Website's name or site's sponsor's name—transition phrase—"quote" - (paragraph symbol paragraph number)

For example: Wikipedia suggests "The Hebrew prophets frequently compared the sin of idolatry to the sin of adultery, in a frequently reappearing rhetorical figure" (¶ 3).

MLA and Paraphrasing

To paraphrase is to restate a passage in *your own* words while keeping the author's ideas intact. In other words, it is to summarize an idea rather than quote it directly.

Author's last name summary (page number)

For example: Vonnegut speaks of human life as being cheap (102).

MLA and the Interview

MLA considers interviews to be recoverable data, so they will be placed on a works cited page. You are to cite them in your text as well, like so:

Interviewee's statement (Interviewee's last name)

"The student was insane to the point of boorishness" (Sideris).

MLA Bibliographical Citation

A bibliography is an *alphabetical* list of citations to books, articles, and other documents found at the end of your paper. An MLA bibliography is called Works Cited. On it, you will list only what you have used in your paper.

Book, Single Author

Baxter, Chet. *Race Equality in Health Care and Education*. New York: Penguin, 1999. Print.

Book, Two Authors

Smith, Gregory, and Tim Johnson. *Your Failure to Please Others*. New York: Harcourt, 2007. Print.

Book, Three or More Authors

Kernis, Mary, Cornell, Dan, and Craig Sun. *Emo: Pure Pretension*. London: Apple, 2004. Print.

Chapter in a Book

Jones, Tom. "Teen Angst." *Textbook of the Misunderstood*. Ed. Jack Holmes. Baltimore: Nova, 2000. 50-62. Print.

Dictionary

"Tambourine." Def. 5b. *The Dictionary of American Music*. 2nd ed. 1990. Print.

Note: Lesser known dictionaries are to include full publication information, with the final result resembling the "chapter in a book" citation described above.

Encyclopedia Entry

"Egoism." *The New Ayn Rand Encyclopedia.* 2nd ed. 1990. Print.

Note: Lesser known encyclopedias are to include full publication information, with the final result resembling the "chapter in a book" citation described above.

Journal Article

Bowles, Anne. "The Psychology of the Spy." *British Journal of Psychiatry* 141.2. Print.

Note: The numbers following the journal's title are the volume and issue numbers, respectfully.

Another Note: Journal articles are referred to as articles, not as "entries." Diaries have entries.

Magazine Article

Benz, Mercedes. "Paris Hilton: The Appeal of Mindlessness." *New Yorker* 7 Oct. 2006: 36-41. Print.

Newspaper Article

Benz, Mercedes. "Paris Hilton: The Appeal of Mindlessness." *Erie Times* 7 Oct. 2006: C12. Print.

Note: Should no author be listed, alphabetize according to article's title.

Holy Book

The New Life Bible. Timothy Johnson, gen. ed. New York: Doubleday, 1985. Print.

Interview

Sideris, Jeremy. 7 July 2007. Phone interview.

Government Document / Pamphlet

United States. Center for Disease Control. *Syphilis is Not an Appropriate Valentine's Day Gift*. Atlanta: Center for Disease Control, 1996. Print.

Electronic Version of a Print Source

Knowles, Beyonce. "How to Get Him to Sweat-out Your Flip." *Urban Inquiry*, 23 Jan. 2004. Web. 15 May 2009.

Article from an Online Dictionary or Encyclopedia

"Mollycoddle." *Encyclopedia Britannica* (1999). n pag. *Encyclopedia Britannica Online*. Web. 15 May 2009.

A Webpage Without an Author

"Better Pickling Methods." Canning Ideas, 2006. Web. 15 May 2009.

A Webpage With an Author

Stewart, Martha. "Better Pickling Methods." Canning Ideas, 23 April 2006. Web. 15 May 2009.

Film

Hip New Teen Movie. Dir. Robert Reed. Perf. Greg Brady and Marsha Brady. Paramount Pictures, 2009. DVD.

Song

Public Enemy. "Night of the Living Baseheads." *It Takes a Nation of Millions to Hold Us Back*. Sony, 1988. CD.

Television Series

"Cliché Premise." *Average Sitcom*. NBC. WBNY, Buffalo. 15 May 2009. Television Broadcast.

Artwork

Vickery Elissa. *Self-portrait*. 2009. Sorbonne Gallery, Paris.

The previous chapter gave attention to a paper's most basic building materials: grammar, paragraph, and citation style. Grammar was reviewed at length because poor grammar use forces a student's public to shift its attention away from the point the student wants to make, and onto the student's errors. Paragraph development's significance was made evident because a student is to write directly and fluidly. Citation style was introduced to the student because the importance of giving credit to another author's ideas found within the student's paper cannot be overemphasized. The next chapter emphasizes revision's leading position within the writing process, and concludes with an array of revision workshop ideas.

Chapter 3
How to Revise a Paper

"There is a level of cowardice lower than that of the
conformist: the fashionable non-conformist."

Ayn Rand

"If only I'd thought of the right words, I could have held on to
your heart. If only I'd thought of the right words, I wouldn't be
breaking apart all my pictures of you."

Robert Smith

What Revision Is

Of the writing process' three stages, revision, the act of making
improvements to your work, is the most important. Yes, prewriting
has its place; you want to outdo your classmates and peers by coming
up with the most original argument. Writing has its use, too. A useful
idea unexpressed is a wasted opportunity to improve the world. Revision, on the other hand, is more important to the writing process than
prewriting and writing are because revision is a recursive endeavor.
Revision forces you to look not only for structural weaknesses in your
essay, but to also revisit often the very quality of your prewriting and
writing efforts. In this way, revision is almost unending; just as you
can always make your argument more original, you can always make
your writing more direct, more fluid. Your essay's due date signals
an end to your essay's revision, but even then, your writing professor
may return your work marked "R&R," as in, "Revise and Resubmit."
Such designation of student work is not uncommon in the Freshman
Composition classroom.

Professional writers are some of the most self-critical people
you will ever meet. You will learn to be strikingly self-critical, too,

when it comes to your own writing. Professional writers base their reputations on their most recent works; whatever recognition their older works brought them simply no longer matters. It will become the same for you. What matters most to your writing professor is the present quality of your work assigned in your Freshman Composition class; that you may have been your high school English teacher's "best student" does not matter to your writing professor in the least. "What have you done for me lately." is a saying that comes to mind. Revision helps you to surpass the quality of your past writing. One way I measure the quality of my students' present work is to take note of what past mistakes and weaknesses they have not repeated.

It is easy to find irony in the Freshman Composition classroom. A number of students, English majors especially, will tell me before their first papers are due that they "work better under pressure [of a deadline]." I, like other writing professors, translate this statement to mean, "Hey, Teach, I am going to write this paper the night before it is due, and there will probably be no time to revise it. That stream of consciousness thing and all that, you know. You're cool with that, right?" After their first papers are handed back the vast majority of these students find they do not, in fact, "work better under pressure." Revision is a cold, harsh mistress. Like paragraph development, she demands a great deal of your time. The sooner you accept this truth, the better. But you are not alone; matter of fact, you are in very good company. If Tom Wolfe, an author known for the thickness of his manuscripts, does not zip his 500 or 600-page first drafts to his publisher for immediate publication without revision, you can afford to spend some quality time with your 5 or 10-page essay.

Revision is a discipline that separates students who come to Freshman Composition with the goal of learning to write well from students who take the class only because it is mandatory. Revision also has something to do with pride. Many students will show they take pride in their writing by fine-tuning their drafts to the best of their abilities, but a few other students without shame will hand-in whatever they have thrown together. Yet other, more melodramatic, students will resist revision altogether because they misguidedly seem to find changing even one word to be an act capable of inflicting the severest emotional damage. Writing well, however, is not a matter of "love me, love my cat" (or my paper); one's public is interested much more in the depth of what one has to say than in any self-described genius of one's writing. It pays not to be too precious. Writing exists first for public education and consumption and second for personal expression. Revision, then, allows us to better serve our various publics.

What You Will Revise, Speaking Generally

In Chapter 2, you were shown how to plan an essay through the development of paragraphs. Paragraphs, I suggested, are the building blocks of any kind of essay you may be called upon to write. How you arrange your paragraphs in an essay, I suggested further, is a question of an essay's form and function. Though you will learn in Freshman Composition that there are many kinds of essays, the important thing to remember is your paragraph outline will provide you with all-important source material that you can shape and revise to suit most any purpose. Now, imagining yourself as a blacksmith with hammer in hand, think of the outlined paragraphs you have accumulated during your prewriting as heated iron ore. The transformation of this imagined ore, in our case the development of your paragraph outline into a specific kind of essay, has as its goal a handiwork capable of not only catching your public's eye, but also worthy of your public's continued use. In short, you are to forge your paragraphs into a revised essay as striking as it is practical. The final appearance that this handiwork, your essay, will conform to is determined by the assignment's instructions your writing professor has outlined for you in your course syllabus. Ideally, instructions found in any Freshman Composition syllabus leave nothing to the students' imagination; however, one finds not all syllabi are of the same quality. Because a student who has been made wholly comfortable with an assignment is a more efficient writer than the student who has not, it is your responsibility to call upon your writing professor to clear-up any vagueness in an assignment's instructions.

What You Will Revise, Speaking Specifically

Professional writers employ two kinds of revision: global and sentence level. Global revision, as the name suggests, refers to double-checking a paper's most important features, and speaks to reexamining the paper as a whole argument. Global revision is interested most in noting the author's adherence to the fundamentals of argument, which I have described earlier in Chapter 1 as: inventio, tempus, stasis, thesis, counter-thesis, ethos, logos, and pathos. Sentence-level revision, on the other hand, refers to double-checking a paper's most basic features, such as the author's grammar use and mastery of citation style. Two concerns, paragraph development and word choice, straddle global and sentence-level revision because they can be analyzed rhetorically and grammatically.

When it comes to applying global and sentence-level revision to your work, balance is of the utmost importance. A strong argument with poor grammar use and little style mastery will sink just as quickly as a flabby argument with excellent grammar use and complete style mastery. What you write and how you write it matters. Your aim is to revise your work until you have produced a strong argument with excellent grammar use and complete style mastery. Below are an array of 12 revision workshop ideas you will use to interrogate your work well before you turn it in. The more revision you do now, the less your writing professor will use his or her red pen later.

Revision Workshop 1, Inventio

You will recall inventio is a Latin word meaning invention or discovery. The term refers to your search for arguments, and you have learned inventio is of primary importance to your paper planning. Inventio reminds you that your argument's success depends largely on your ability to imagine any question your public may have. The more you anticipate your public's concern, the more persuasive your argument will be. It is seldom the known question that devastates your argument; rather, it is the question that you have not considered that makes your argument seem half-baked and untrustworthy. Use the following inventio-related questions to measure the quality of your search for arguments.

1. Exactly how did I detect the idea my public has not yet considered?
    a. Was my detection a matter of guesswork or research?
2. Exactly how did I expect my public to receive my idea?
    a. Was my expectation based on imagination or observation?
3. Exactly how did I learn what my public already knows about my topic?
    a. Was my research primary or secondary?
4. Exactly how did I estimate the impact my argument will have on my public?
    a. Was my estimation optimistic or pessimistic?
5. Exactly how did I define the words most important to my argument?
    a. Were my definitions colloquial or research based?

Holding your paper up to the light offered by the inventio-related questions above helps you to determine if your argument is based on your assumptions or on a reality you share with your public. An argument based on your assumptions alone is a tough road to hoe because it compels your public to trust you from the very start, something it may not be willing to do. Conversely, an argument based squarely on a reality shared with your public endeavors to build trust quickly. Because you make yourself recognized as "one of them," your argument appears to your public, at least at first, as much less of an unknown quantity, and subsequently, more worthy of its initial trust.

Revision Workshop 2, Tempus

I have informed you tempus is a Latin word for time. While inventio helps you search for original arguments and assists in planning your paper's content, tempus allows you to judge how timely your argument is. Again, timely refers to introducing an argument *ad tempus*, at the most correct moment. The importance of your argument's timeliness cannot be overstated; your decision when to introduce an argument will make you appear to your public as a leader or as a lemming. Use the tempus-related prompts below to judge the timeliness of your argument.

1. My idea came to me completely on my own.
- If so, you are a trendsetter, and your argument is timely, indeed.
2. My idea came to me as a response to something I heard in a class.
- Your professor is up on things, so your argument fits in nicely with the conversation.
3. My idea came to me as a response to something I read in a book.
- A book can be timeless, so it is possible some new argument may yet be invented.
4. My idea came to me as a response to something I read in a journal.
- Journals are known for publishing research breakthroughs, but why piggyback?
5. My idea came to me as a response to something I read in a magazine.
- The news in a magazine may have a definite shelf life, and your argument might, too.
6. My idea came to me as a response to something I heard or read on the Internet, news, radio, or television.
- You, my friend, have become a slave to the news cycle. Try again.

I would do well to repeat an earlier word of caution here. The strong emphasis this book places on an idea's timeliness and originality does not suggest you ought to disregard the value of secondary or book research. On the contrary, the more knowledgeable you make yourself on a topic, the more trust the public will place in your argument. Further, once you have used secondary research to learn what was been said about a topic, you will be far less likely to mimic ideas belonging to others.

Revision Workshop 3, Stasis

Remember stasis? No, it has nothing to do with Stacey, your good friend from around the way. Stasis is a Greek word meaning standing still, and it refers to the opinion or standpoint upon which your argument is built. Stasis is central to the development of your paper's argument. The result of not knowing precisely where you stand on an issue during the planning of your work is an essay that lacks focus. Use the following stasis-related questions to measure the strength of your opinion.

1. Have I described all of the facts pertaining to my argument?
   a. Did I consider *all* points of view against my argument?
2. Have I described the motivation behind my argument?
   a. Did I give my public my argument's exact context or historical background?
3. Have I described the effects of my argument?
   a. Did I list each of my argument's goals?
4. Have I described the significance of my argument?
   a. Did I inform my public what will happen if my call to action is not acted upon?
5. Have I described a solution to the problem my argument has exposed?
   a. Did I state what should be done, and what is the best way to do it?

Remembering a stasis is viewed best as an argument in embryonic form, the questions above allow you to see how close to term your argument is.

Revision Workshop 4, Thesis

When I spoke of thesis in Chapter 1, I referred to it as an all-important position statement, an essential, precise, guiding sentence that you will defend in each of your paper's paragraphs. Moreover, I said if you take anything from our thesis review, take this: the more original your argument is, the more your public will have to pay attention to you; your unique idea will be difficult to challenge because you will have made yourself the sole authority on the matter. Use the thesis-related checklist below to judge the precision of your argument.

1. My thesis statement does not end with a question mark.
2. My thesis statement does not include phrases, such as "I think," "I feel," or "I believe."
3. My thesis statement does not include the unnecessary phrase, "I argue that."
4. My thesis statement does not include a quote.
5. My thesis statement does not include vague language.
6. My thesis statement contains as many words from my taxonomy as possible.
7. My thesis statement contains an original point.
8. My thesis statement contains momentum.
9. My thesis statement contains enough ammunition for several paragraphs.
10. My thesis statement contains a sense of hope.

Do not underestimate the worth of a good thesis statement. Speaking frankly, the thesis statement is what I read first when I set about evaluating a student's work. Within moments of reading it I know whether I have something thoughtful and exciting on my desk or if I have stumbled upon a radical new cure for insomnia.

Revision Workshop 5, Counter-thesis

Counter-thesis-related activities are fun because they force you to think on your feet. You will remember counter-thesis is another word for counter-argument, and both speak to tackling and reconciling *all* points of view opposing your thesis statement. I have asked you to consider two chief varieties of counter-theses when you plan your paper: arguments that contradict your point of view and your arguments that contradict the points of view presented by other authors. Use the following counter-thesis-related checklist to: 1) note how well you have challenged and neutralized your opposition's thesis statements, and 2) note how well you have prepared your thesis statement's defenses.

1. Have I stated exactly who opposes my argument?
2. Have I stated exactly what is incorrect in my opposition's writing?
3. Have I stated exactly when or where my opposition is incorrect?
4. Have I stated exactly why or how my opposition is incorrect?
5. Have I determined why others oppose my argument?
6. Have I determined what others view as my argument's failings?
7. Have I determined when or where others can breach my argument?
8. Have I determined how others can breach my argument?
9. Have I cheapened myself, and weakened my position, with name-calling or insinuation?
10. Have I cheapened myself, and weakened my position, by employing stereotypes?

Do not assume your argument is unassailable. There is a counter-thesis for every thesis, and a sincere opponent for every sincere proponent.

Revision Workshop 6, Ethos

Ethos, defined in Chapter 1 as character, credibility, and reputation, is key to your identity as a writer. A strong ethos suggests to your public you are serious, believable, and worthy of respect. Conversely, a weak ethos suggests to your public you are, at best, a well-intentioned buffoon, and at worst, a phony or a raving loon. What of a middling ethos? Forget about it. Who wants to be viewed as half-serious, almost believable, and near worthy of respect? Answer the questions below to measure your level of ethos.

1. Where have I shown myself to be an expert on my topic?
2. Where have I shown practicality in my writing?
3. Where have I shown greater emphasis on actual reality and less emphasis on theoretical reality in my writing?
4. Where have I shown myself to be fully aware of how things are today from my public's perspective?
5. Where have I shown I have my public's best interests at heart?
6. Where have I shown attention to my public's immediate needs?
7. Where have I shown attention to my public's long-term needs?
8. Where have I shown my public I come as a friend?
9. Where have I shown my public I will not play the scold?
10. Where have I shown my public I will not scapegoat anyone?
11. Where have I shown my public all may share in the brighter future my argument suggests?

Ethos, then, is a synthesis of many virtues: knowledge balanced by wisdom, optimism balanced by common sense, and activism balanced by friendship.

Revision Workshop 7, Logos

You have likely found logos (i.e. word, text, reason) to be the most abstract of all of the concepts presented to you in this text. While grammar reminds you of the importance of proper word choice, logos calls upon you to select the very best word to convey your exact meaning. Logos also calls upon you to make use of the best outside research as an important means of lending support to your argument. Logos further reminds you to employ the language and a manner of presentation most appropriate for your public. The link between word and figurative language (e.g. metaphor, simile) is logos' domain, too. Use the Orwell-inspired checklist below to judge the extent of your paper's logos.

1.   I have removed all commonly heard phrases.
2.   I have removed all longer words and replaced them with their shorter synonyms.
3.   I have removed all unnecessary words.
4.   I have removed all euphemisms and vague words.
5.   I have removed all passive voice and replaced it with active voice.
6.   I have removed all buzz (jargon) words and replaced them with lay English.
7.   I have removed all quotes not absolutely necessary to the point I am making.
8.   I have removed all quotes taken from authors who possess little ethos.
9.   I have removed all language that distances me from my public.

Logos demands you trim all of the fat from your paper. You are to write directly, and with as few words as possible.

Revision Workshop 8, Pathos

Again, pathos is used to provoke a tangible feeling within your public. You are to place pathos into your writing with precision. Using pathos expertly is a matter of planning what exact emotions you want your public to feel, and knowing specifically where to encourage these emotions for greatest persuasive effect. Too many beginning writers forget the importance of stimulating their readers. Rather than composing exciting page-turners, many students play it more than safe, and consequently, turn in work that informs, but does not live. It is your mission to move your public to feel something far beyond boredom. Use the questions below to measure the strength of your pathos.

1. What mood did I set for my public in my introductory paragraph?
    a. What words and phrases lent most to this mood?
    b. What words and phrases lent least to this mood?
2. Where in my essay did I reinforce this mood?
    a. Where did I place my set-ups?
    b. Where did I place my punch lines or climactic phrases?
3. Where in my essay did I let up on this mood?
    a. Where did I give my audience breathers?
    b. Did these breathers strengthen my next punch line or climactic phrase?
4. What mood did I set for my public in my concluding paragraph?
    c. Did this final mood assist persuading my public to act on my call to action?
    d. Was this final mood a feeling my public can appreciate?

Humans are emotional animals, and your writing has to appeal as much to the heart as it does to the head. Pathos reminds us there are no boring subjects, only boring writers.

Revision Workshop 9, Grammar

You have learned grammar helps to organize your thoughts. A paper that does not employ grammar to full effect will not be understood, and it will fail to be persuasive. Grammar also adds simple elegance to your paper. The expertise with which you shape your words, sentences, and paragraphs is equal to poise. The more easily your writing moves, the less clumsy your thinking appears. Like logos, grammar is interested in applying the ideal word and the ideal punctuation at the ideal time. The sooner you study grammar choices made by professional writers, the sooner your grammar level will catch up with that of your more educationally-privileged classmates. Use the checklist below to judge the grace of your paper's grammar.

1. I did not write like I speak.
   a. I have reminded myself that unlike speaking, writing is a careful, unhurried, objective expression of my thought.
2. I have left my home dialect at home.
   a. I have reminded myself though everyone possesses home dialects, I have avoided using mine so as not to distance myself from the public.
3. I did not take the easy way out.
   a. I have reminded myself to avoid using contractions and Text Speak, and I have made sure my paper does not have one spelling error.
4. I have taken note of how my favorite authors have used grammar.
   a. I have reminded myself though it is important for me to develop my own writer's voice, observing my favorite authors' syntax can be constructive.
5. I have taken my rough draft to my university's writing center several times for revision.
   a. I have reminded myself the more sets of trained eyes I ask to look at my paper, the more grammatical errors will be found and eliminated.

Your first goal in Freshman Composition is to avoid making the same errors found in your high school writing. Like other writing professors, I prefer my students to make new grammatical mistakes than repeat the old. One cannot progress if one is stuck in the past.

Revision Workshop 10, Citation Style

You have been given three reasons to cite work and ideas belonging to other authors: 1) citations give authors credit where credit is due; 2) citations join your paper to the works of established authors explicitly; and 3) citations make it easy for your readers to collect the materials you have cited for themselves. You will find revision activities related to citation style are so easy they almost insult your intelligence; citation, after all, is interested much more in conformity than in imagination. One finds six prompts related to citation style revision:

1. Each of my citations contains the exact information called for by the citation style I have used, and I have placed this information in the order called for exactly.
2. Each of my citations pays strict attention to the punctuation called for by the citation style I have used.
3. Each of my quotations and paraphrases has been given a citation.
4. Each of my quotations and paraphrases is sandwiched by introductory and explanatory sentences.
5. Each of my paper's parts (e.g. body and bibliography) uses the same citation style.
6. Each of the book and journal title I have referenced is italicized, and each chapter and journal article title is placed in quotation marks.
7. Each act of plagiarism is an exciting opportunity to be expelled from university.

A point I brought up in Chapter 2 bears repetition: professors take their pet citation styles' appearances very seriously, and many students' papers have failed as a result of careless style application. Given how easy citation style is to apply, mistakes with its application can be ascribed to sheer laziness.

Revision Workshop 11, Paragraph Development

At heart, paragraph development is all about planning your line of attack. Paragraph development is a matter of knowing when and where you will introduce and reinforce your ideas. You have learned previously the best tool for paragraph development is the outline. The more substantial you make your outline, the less you will struggle when you draft your paper. Like word choice, paragraph development can be analyzed rhetorically and grammatically. Use the checklist below to: 1) note how substantial your paragraphs are, and 2) note how well your paragraphs flow.

1. My introductory paragraph has seven parts:
    a. A topic sentence
    b. Ideas related to the need for my argument
    c. Ideas related to the significance of my argument
    d. Ideas related to the history of my argument
    e. Ideas related to the words most important to my argument
    f. Ideas related to the prejudice I brought to my argument
    g. A thesis statement
2. Each of my body paragraphs has four or five parts:
    a. A topic sentence that refers back to the paper's thesis while it suggests its paragraph's content
    b. Primary examples and ideas
    c. Secondary examples and ideas
    d. Tertiary examples and ideas, if needed
    e. A transition sentence that concludes the idea housed in its paragraph's body while it suggests the next paragraph's content
3. My body paragraph with a quote has seven or eight parts:
    a. A topic sentence that refers back to the paper's thesis while it suggests its paragraph's content
    b. Primary examples and ideas
    c. Secondary examples and ideas

      i.   Introduction to quotation
      ii.   Quotation
      iii. Explanation of quotation
  d. Tertiary examples and ideas, if needed
  e. A transition sentence that concludes the idea housed in its paragraph's body while it suggests the next paragraph's content

4. My concluding paragraph has five parts:
  a. A reworded thesis statement
  b. A restatement of my paper's goals
  c. A description of my paper's findings
  d. A description of my paper's limitations
  e. A description of my paper's implications on future research in the same subject area

Each of your paragraphs is to fit together seamlessly. Again, it will help you to imagine sentences and paragraphs as Lego construction bricks and your outline as a blueprint.

Revision Workshop 12, Word Choice

Finding the right word to say is no matter of luck. Rather, your word choice is to be deliberate, and the result of much work. Do not confuse the application of proper word choice with loading your paper with flowery language; a thesaurus is not always your best friend. There is no need, for instance, to write "chartreuse" when "light green" will do. Avoid vague word choices like euphemisms, too (e.g. "pass" for die, "voluptuous" for obese). Remember, the more plainly you speak, the larger your readership will be. The beauty and power of words should be self-evident, and flash is no substitute for substance. Below are tips that will help you avoid the most common word choice mistakes students make:

- Do not confuse "then" and "than." Then refers to sequence, as in, "I went to class, and then I went to the gym." Than refers to quantity, as in, "I ate more pizza than you." Given these pointers, the sentence, "I ate more pizza then you" is awkward, indeed.

- Do not confuse "there" and "their." There speaks to direction (remember, there has "here" in it). Their speaks to possession. For example, "Their pizza is over there."

- Do not confuse "affect," a verb, and "effect," a noun. Note their correct uses: "My all-night partying affected my schoolwork, and the effect was I had to drop out of school."

- Do not confuse "this," a singular pronoun, with its plural form, "these." This is a mistake common to my students whose first language is Spanish, as their accents sometimes transform a soft I sound into a long E sound.

- Do not mix and match singular nouns and plural pronouns. A singular noun is to be followed by a singular pronoun, and a plural noun is to be followed by a plural pronoun. The sentence, "A student should bring their pencil" does not make sense because "a" refers to one student, and "their" refers to more than one student. You can revise this sentence while keeping its spirit by writing, "Students should bring their pencils"

Words are to a sentence as bricks are to a wall. Misplaced words, or bricks, lead to structural uncertainty.

In the preceding chapter, light was shed on revision, the most important of the writing process' three stages. Attention given to global and sentence-level revision took the form of 12 workshops. The next chapter, "Select Examples of Student Writing", provides two representative examples of student writing: "Meaningful lives of the undead: A deeper look into the substantiveness of the modern gothic lifestyle", a paper based on secondary research, and "Disabling misconceptions: A study on the dating practices of physically disabled women and able-bodied men", a paper based on primary and secondary research.

Chapter 4
Select Examples of Student Writing

"A kiss must be understood as the pressing together of two alimentary canals."

Sigmund Freud

"Imagination is more important than knowledge."

Albert Einstein

In any given semester I grade about 500 papers (4 classes x 25 students per class x 5 papers assigned to each student). I am thus assured a wide variety of student writing will make it to my desk. Profound papers will find themselves next to superficial papers, and extraordinary ideas will make themselves known to me as much as insignificant ideas will. Given the sheer diversity of student work I have encountered (I have taught for 10 years), selecting examples of student writing for this textbook was difficult. I did not want to include the most complex papers I have read because all who read these example papers must feel able to imitate the quality of the sampled work. I had no interest in including simplistic student work, either, because the textbook's readers ought to see what excellent writing can look like so they may endeavor to match it.

I have chosen to include the following papers because the thinking in them is original, and the way they are written is thoughtful. Like the greatest researchers, these student authors were not content to retread familiar subjects. On the contrary, they redefined our collective reality by shedding light upon new ideas; they chose to explore the unknown rather than act as Sunday day trippers at a chardonnay tasting. I know you will enjoy reading these papers as much as did I.

Meaningful lives of the undead:
A deeper look into the substantiveness of the modern gothic lifestyle

Alyssa Florentine, Nicole Tonty, Donald Wisniewski
English 102: Specialized Writing and Research Skills
Dr. Jeremy Sideris
March 9, 2009

Abstract

The purpose of this paper is to suggest "Goth" is a more substantive lifestyle choice than "Emo." Over the past few years there has been a misunderstanding of the two lifestyles, and many people have confused them as being exactly the same. The truth, however, is that they are two very different ways of living. This paper will suggest the "Goth" lifestyle choice is one in which a person's whole life is consumed with the elements of the culture compared to the "Emo" lifestyle, which is still being formed by teens who do not know how to express their emotions.

Over the course of researching this topic we have looked through fashion and music, magazines, books, journals, newspaper articles, and even news broadcasts. Almost all of the sources seem to say the same thing: "Goth" is a lifestyle and a culture that people hold on to forever and live by, and "Emo" is a teen fad gone wrong. Both lifestyles are centered basically on the music which represents them and both types of music are dark and dreary. Some of the songs share the same beat and delivery of lyrics, but the difference lies in the actual lyrics of the songs. Fashion plays an important role in both cultures as well, being used to define who that person is. The styles are very different and seem to tell a lot about that person's view of society and view of themselves.

Our findings were quite concrete; however, in some sources there was some contradiction. It seems no one can agree on a set standard of what exactly "Goth" and "Emo" are. So as it stands, an objective research method was employed and every finding was double checked with another source.

Meaningful lives of the undead:
A deeper look into the substantiveness of the modern gothic lifestyle

In this research paper it is important to define elements of the topic. To examine whether the "Emo" or "Goth" subculture proves to be a more substantive lifestyle, one must define the meaning of substantive. According to the *Oxford American College Dictionary* (Lindberg, 2002, p. 1375) the adjective means, "1. Having a firm basis in reality and so important or meaningful. 2. Having a separate and independent existence." These meanings are similar, yet, when applied to a lifestyle, can be taken in completely different directions.

We will investigate "Goth" and "Emo" positions in reality, as well as their importance and meaning. In the research process, there are many credible sources such as books and journals analyzing the gothic subculture written by credible authors. Whereas in the research for the "Emo" subculture, most sources were primarily created by the members of the "Emo" community. With further investigation, it is clear the "Goth" scene is more of a developed subculture, while "Emo" only pertains to style and music. As for the question of their strength in society, the "Goth" subculture seems to have a hold while "Emo" slips by the wayside.

This paper covers the aspects of music, fashion, and the overall view of society in the "Goth" and "Emo" subcultures. It is apparent that music plays an important role in both of these subcultures. According to the *Oxford American College Dictionary*, one definition for "Goth" is, "1. A style of rock music derived from punk, typically with apocalyptic or mystical lyrics" (Lindberg, 2002, p. 1375). Music is a way of expressing emotion and ideas. The style of music listened to by "Goths" varies just as much as they do, but it is based mostly on rock beats and rhythms. "Goth" bands center on a few main topics, such as the occult, perverse sex and vampirism, but there are many more (Brill, 2008). The purpose of their music is to question ideas and challenge powers in a time when everything is uncertain. Most songs are based on world events or a specific message the artist is trying to get across (Brill, 2008). "Emo" music is very different in style and in the message they intend to send. The music that "Emo" people listen to is basically a cry for help. The lyrics talk about committing suicide, cutting, hating life, hating the world, and for others to notice how miserable they are (Sands, 2006, p. 2). For them, music is another way to express their emotions apart from cutting and suicide attempts. Overall, "Goth" music is generally more accepted in everyday culture and is used in many movies, commercials and other television shows (Bark, n.d., pp. 24-25).

Fashion is also an important part of both of these subcultures that really helps to set them apart from each other and from other subcultures. Another definition of "Goth" given by *The Oxford American College Dictionary* (2002) is "1. A member of a subculture favoring black clothing, white and black makeup, and "Goth" music" (p. 1375) . Fashion for "Goths" differs between each person. The standard trends that research has suggested is a pale face, eyes and lips black, corsets, capes, Celtic Crosses, etc. (Sands, 2006, p. 1). Fashion for "Emos" is not just about the clothes. Their style varies from bright colored shirts to dark. Very tight pants are worn and everyone is extremely skinny. In her article, Sands (2006) explains that "Emo" kids "show inner despair by looking like you are too sad to eat. Obesity and emocity do not mix" (p. 2). This is a very interesting point she makes, arguing that being very thin is a part of the style. Taken as a whole, fashion marks the major difference between the two subcultures.

Outsiders to the "Goth" subculture would have a hard time understanding why they dress the way they do and listen to the music they do. "Goths" usually become gothic because they have been shunned by society; they feel they do not fit in. Some sources described the gothic community as being individuals who share a common dissatisfaction toward society (Eider, 2001, ¶ 3). This subculture is used as an outlet for society's outsiders who do not live their lives the way other people are told to (Farkas, 2006, p. 31).

From the sources investigated, it seems as if outsiders do not understand the major differences that separate the two subcultures. Information from sources proved not to be credible by confusing "Goth" and "Emo." Some even said they are the same thing. This argument is important because society needs to understand the differences between "Goth" and "Emo" styles.

According to Sands (2006), the point of distinction between the two subcultures is "a celebration of self harm" (p. 1). This is a scary and alarming truth for parents and teachers who may not be equipped to deal with children with these kinds of problems. Her article goes on to suggest "Emo" kids exchange competitive messages on their blogs about the scars on their wrists and the best way to display them (Sands, 2006, p. 2). There was no information found on "Goths" celebrating self mutilation, blogging about ways to show off their individuality, nor anything about how "Goth" they are. This information is provided to inform parents and teachers of the differences between the "Goth" and "Emo" subcultures, how to let them know if they should be worried, and how to help these individuals.

The people who seem to get the most upset about this discussion are the "Emo" kids. After reading comments left on articles and news reports, it started to seem they were upset by the way people stereotyped them and all of the misconceptions these articles reported. This comment, made by a very irate "Emo," was left on a website that archived a news report called "I Must Be Emo" (2007):

> u no wat emos r not pathetic k bitch they r not stupid they r not a fukinload of crap they hav feelings 2 they r human 2 ppl shouldn't fukin bitch around w emo cuz if u were emo n ppl wer doin dat 2 u u would b fukin piss so shut da fuk up u fukin bitches fags douchbags etc this is a fucked up video u don't know how us emos feel if u thk emos r weird gay wateva u r so fucked up. (Dullum, 2007, comment #45)

This news report explains the "Emo" culture and some fads that are running through schools. It expresses concern and a warning for all parents to look out for children who may be falling into an "Emo" lifestyle.

"Goths," on the other hand, do not seem to mind reports and articles on their subculture. In researching, there were no books that said they did not mind it, but from looking at blogs and news reports where there is room to leave comments there were none made by any angry "Goths". The "Goth" subculture is very old and complex, and so far sources have told us "Goth" is a complete lifestyle whereas "Emo" is just music and clothing (Popkin, 2006, p. 1).

The impact of this debate is one that could potentially eliminate a subculture altogether. Many of these sources call the "Emo" people out on not being a part of a real subculture, saying that they mix different fads from other subcultures and will join any group they can fit in. A great deal of research and critical thinking is involved because "Goth" has a more defined subculture.

Literature Review

According to the web community Goth.net (2001), the biggest part of being "Goth" is sharing the common dissatisfaction toward society. Elder (2001) states, "Most Goths become Goths because they have been spurned by 'normal' society because the way want to live their lives does not fit in with how people are told to live theirs" (¶ 3). This standpoint toward society that "Goths" possess is what "Emos" lack. Riggs (2008) finds in his research, "Emos don't qualify as an urban tribe because they are too con-sumerist and lack a social or political philosophy" (p. 40). Farkas (2006) describes the gothic community as an aid for society's misfits to better define themselves as well as others. In response to this research, the two groups share social rebellious tendencies, but where "Emo" is mainly emotionally charged and self-motivated defense, "Goth" is a group-oriented offense against society.

Through the examination of the "Goth" subculture's role in society, the unity and groupthink of the "Goths" is what sustains the group's importance in society. Considering the second definition of "substantive," the findings in the previous research contradict the ideas of having independence. Simultaneously, it is hard to say "Emo" subculture has a sufficient backbone to support itself, either. Myerson (2000) states Transcendentalist intellectuals, such as Thoreau and Emerson, would say self-sufficiency is the way to achieve enlightenment. This self-sufficiency was thought to be achieved through breaking free from the holds of society. Yet in the book, *Evil Inside*

Human Violence and Cruelty, Baumeister (1997) explains, it is human nature to need the feeling of attachment to a particular group. The "Goth" culture can be compared to the transcendental movement; both share the common hatred for society, yet both groups exist primarily because of their relationship counterpart, society.

Although previous research proves the gothic community to be dependent within as well as on society, for its purpose, it seems gothic individuals' original intent was self-sufficiency. Hodkinson (2002) observed during his research interviews the "Goth" subjects defended their lifestyles, identifying them as an act of individualism. He makes his case when he points out their obvious conformity to specific group identities. When asked the question, "In your own words, please explain what the "Goth" scene is all about," the respondent answers, "Having the absolute freedom to dress as you want and to express yourself as you want" (¶ 25).

Contradictory to proclamations of this gothic individual, many gothic communities, web-based or otherwise, will actually present a checklist of the steps to becoming "Goth". In the *Washington Post*, Peter Carlson (2007) examines the role of fashion in the "Goth" culture. He determines, just as the regular fashion world shifts and changes, so does the gothic fashion realm. Upon concluding the article, he includes a list of "25 bits of stage advice" from the self-proclaimed "Hollywood's Legendary Gothic/Death Rock Band," the Astrovamps. These tips include: "Always wear Eyeliner. Blue-jeans are a Goth Fashion sin. For lipstick and nail polish, black and blood red are the only colors you'll ever need" (¶ 16). Their tips are, more or less, orders to a "Goth", which following will result in the advisee to appear more "Goth". Hodkinson (2002) concludes his findings in his interview-conducted research:

> The somewhat one-dimensional sense of identity and distinction held by many, the way in which Goths so frequently positioned themselves against those they perceived as 'trendies' is significant in that it implies they also shared a set of moral assumptions about their lifestyle which allowed many of them to understand it as culturally superior. These I shall refer to as the *ideals* of the subculture. (¶ 15)

Another example of this contradiction of individuality is exemplified on for "Goth" created by "Goth" web community sites. On the site Goth.net, Preston Eider (2008) speaks on behalf of "Goths" in showing discontentment for the stereotypes of "Goths" by style, music, and religious beliefs. After addressing this he follows this section with ways to get into the "Goth" scene, where he explains the style, music scene, and even sense of humor one needs to become a part of the "Goth" community. Where "Goth" thrives in community, the "Emo" subculture may lack. The lack of philosophy and view towards society discussed earlier in Rigg's (2006) findings does not mean "Emos" flourish independence. The site for "Emos" created by "Emos", Emo-Corner.com (2008), contains narrow rules for "Emos" to follow regarding style, music, and behavior. The only individual aspect is the extreme emotionally-charged attitude, which is in no way a self-sufficient lifestyle. The issue being addressed through research analysis is, using the first definition of substantive, "Goths" pose a more substantive lifestyle compared to "Emo," but to justify the substantiveness of "Goth" lifestyle, one must consider all aspects of what it means to live substantively.

In the development of this research, one must consider the two characteristics of the two subcultures which identify them apart from society. Their emphasis on style and music in the gothic subculture has developed a fashion culture of their own. Concentrated around the music scene, the style has shifted and adapted into many different genres of "Goth" within the "Goth" culture. Brill (2008) describes the origin of the modern gothic subculture as a hazy combination of influences pulled from music, fashion, literature, and art. Creators of Darkindeoendent.net suggest the dark style stems from the gothic English literature movement dating back to the 1700's. This explains the black clothing as well as the fascination with the dark, taboo subjects. An interesting comparison is found in Carlson's (2007) article in *The Washington Post*. In his interview, editors from *Gothic Beauty* magazine are saying gothic fashion has taken a turn from the old Victorian gothic style to a new "futuristic science fiction" era. The important mentality is to recognize "Goth" as more than just a fad. While considered in a subset of punk rock, "Goth" rock and industrial music can still be found in wide circulation today, which will be investigated further in our research. "Gothic subculture has not only remained in existence, it had also changed, evolved and separated into various branches. Perhaps the reason behind this...Death and decay are concepts which are both universally applicable and constant" (Beneath-Lui, 2008, ¶ 5).

Much of the "Emo" subculture's stems from trends set by the "Goth" fashion. Luv-Emo.com (2007) self-proclaims the "Emo" subculture's roots as being solely derived from the 1980's punk style. The rest of their influence comes from within the group. These are interesting observations being compared: if substantive means having a firm basis in reality, "Goth" would be considered more substantive with influences coming from many different sources and time eras. If substantive means having a separate independent existence, "Emos" fashion and music is much more substantive.

Although both groups have a style, it is clear "Goth" style has a much broader spectrum of trends within their culture's fashion scene. "Emo" has a narrow selection of trends making individuality a little harder to achieve within the group. This is identified through the "Emo" websites such as Luv-emo (2007) and Emo corner (2008) which have guidelines on how to wear hair, makeup and clothing. Carlson's (2008) article on "Goths" reveals the diversity of style within the "Goth" subculture.

On Goth.net, Eider (2001) describes "Goths" as not having a particular music to follow but also credits '80's punk bands as the founders of "Goth." He goes on to explain ways to be more involved in the "Goth" culture such as through the club scene, which draws in the "Goths" through their common love for gothic music. Brill (2008) explains gothic music as a parallel to gothic fashion; there are many shades to the "Goth" music spectrum. Artists including Rammstein, Marilyn Manson, Evanescence, Type O Negative, and Rob Zombie are some of the better known within this scene. The music could be full of angry stabbing sounds giving the feeling of darkness and destruction. There is the industrial music branch containing harsh sounds of machinery work. Gothic individuals seem to identify gothic music as their own preference, within guidelines of course. Many artists, such as Marilyn Manson, Evanescence and Nine Inch Nails, gain popularity within and outside the "Goth" culture. The reason for this intermixing of popular culture and "Goth" culture is, "Goth" music has no specific genre of its own, and it contains genres within itself. Brill (2008) explains the criteria for "Goth" music to be accepted by the "Goth" culture: it must portray a sense of contempt for the larger society.

"Goth" and "Emo" music are both represented mainly through lyrics. Similar to the two subcultures' societal stance, "Goth" lyrics express an offensive approach, embracing the undead and challenging the norms, and "Emo" lyrics cry a defensive approach through self-pity and grief. According to Popkin (2006), the subculture's name is a result of Minor Threat's front man, MacKaye, self mocking after a betrayed fan had called him "emocore" (¶ 7). The punk fans of these evolving "Emo" bands criticized their new emotional expressive approach, which only fueled their emotionally charged experimentation, turning into a hate for the rest of adult society. The misunderstood defense attracts mainly young adults going through puberty. Riggs (2008) poses the important question, "What could be easier for a teenager to love—and to hate—than a movement reflecting the confusion lifestyle. The "Emo" individuals depend on others to blame for their emotional angst, which gives society an important role on the subcultures main philosophy."

Both "Goth" and "Emo" cultures struggle with accepting the importance of society's role present in their philosophy. Wittaker (2007) explains how many individuals of subcultures choose to reject society completely. These extreme individuals block out the world and retreat to the Internet. Because of this, "Goth" and "Emo" cultures flourish throughout cyberspace. This creates a group, even for extremely isolated individuals. Incidents like the shooting at Columbine have been credited to and influenced by the "Goth" culture, similar to the ways cutting and self-harm have been blamed on the "Emo" subculture. This is where both groups are seen as threatening to the norm.

Rutledge (2008) warns adults of the "Goth" and "Emo" subcultures, claiming them high- risk cultures. She accuses "Goth" and

"Emo" subcultures as the source for most teen depression, violence, suicide and psychological risks. "Goth" and "Emo" responses all over the Internet defend themselves by saying their subcultures attract misfits but do not encourage them. It is these individuals who lack substance in their lives, who give them a bad reputation. Robinson (2008) defends "Goths" on religoustolerance.org, saying that "Goth" lifestyle does not encourage violence and Satanism. Robinson states, "Goth music often deals with thought-provoking topics, concentrating on societal evils like racism, war, hatred or groups, etc. Their music tends to concentrate on the very *"nasty unhappy'* topics that *North American* culture wants to *ignore and forget*" (¶ 7). These two arguments have the ability to either make or break the "Goth" culture as a substantive lifestyle. As for the "Emo" subculture, Riggs (2008) points out that the danger is the combination of the embracing of painful self-pity and lack of mature philosophical outlook. The combination of these elements causes a group's original purpose to be lost, and in turn, strips the substantiveness from the lifestyle.

Eider (2001) speaks on behalf of the entire "Goth" subculture when he explains the gothic philosophy of acceptance, and open-mindedness to others. From this, he infers the gothic lifestyle draws in a large population for society's misfits, which often gives an angry outcast a place of belonging. Brill (2008) finds in his own research, for the same reason discussed, many members of the homosexual community are drawn to the gothic lifestyle. Because there is now a gothic bond between all homosexuals, heterosexuals, and genders within the subculture, the line separating gender roles becomes a dark blur. "Goths often portray their scene as a haven of free-floating bisexual desire, as something like 'genderless' spaces where partners are chosen for their looks and character, regardless of gender" (p. 124). This is an aspect of the gothic culture which allows it to stand on its own. Members of the groups are able to intermingle and experience sexual relationships with any member, without ever having to look beyond the group. The opposing "Emo" group tries to experiment with gender by mixing the clothing style, but lack a philosophy of sexuality.

Discussion

When placed side by side, these two life styles seemingly have much in common. Both take their base from the musical style for which they are named. The public outlook on these groups represents them as dark and depressed people, with a suicidal or violent personality. This is not true of the groups.

The research into the "Goth" and "Emo" styles was hard to get started. This shortcoming was due to not knowing under which classification of books to look for information, or proper publications that fit within the given scope of acceptable material. Once materials were acquired, it was an issue of the negative stance that is taken on the "Emo" culture.

Music of the "Goth" and "Emo"

The "Goth" culture is based in its entirety around the music that represents them. The styles in which it is written and played vary like the artists themselves. Many have found their way into the pop culture without placing forth the effort. Often times it is heard in the movies during a dramatic moment; when you hear the driving beat of the drums and cannot discern a melody, it is then you are hearing a piece of "Goth" music.

The categories of "Goth" music are based mostly around rock beats and rhythms. Many artists that fall into the assorted categories in which "Goth" can be placed are surprising. A complete listing of these bands would undoubtedly take several volumes to list, along with their songs. One common thread of the topics which they cover: nothing is seemingly taboo; the occult, perverse sex and vampirism name only a few.

This element of the music leads to the discussion of who is then considered to be a "Goth" artist completely and those who are only in the presence briefly. Acts like Marilyn Manson, Rob Zombie, Evanescence, Nine Inch Nails, and Type O Negative seem to fill into that gap created. From what is discernable, however, Rob Zombie is kept off the list by many; this may be due to the heavy metal nature of the music and the search for traditional categorization.

With the inclusion of "Goth" music into mainstream media, it plays out as a passive form of acceptance of the culture, but a level of misunderstanding still exists. Listen to the Howard Stern show and you will hear them return from commercial or go to commercial by playing the musical riff to "Feel So Numb" by Rob Zombie (2001). Go to the end scene in the movie *House on Haunted Hill* (1999) and you hear Marilyn Manson's cover of the song "Sweet Dreams" (1994). The use of music stylized in the manner provides dramatic elements that may fill a sequence better than the traditional composed music can cover in the vision of the director, or it may be completely out of place for the style of movie.

The purpose of the music claims to be a questioning of ideas and long held beliefs. To challenge the powers that be in a time when everything else is uncertain is an understandable act, but that does not make their motives pure. Many artists are found mired in controversy, and the level to which it is known varies based on current world events and what everyone is talking about. Most everyone knows of the great controversy that wrapped around Marilyn Manson after the shootings in Columbine. It was said his music led to their actions, and he should be held accountable for what they did. The truth is we are in an era in which violence and intolerance are allowed to go unchecked due to laws so vague most parents are unwilling to discipline their children for fear of being arrested for child abuse. To that end the blame should fall at the feet of our elected officials; however, that is another paper's topic.

The music itself sounds more introverted in nature, much like the people of the "Goth" lifestyle and culture it represents. Your introverted person is more likely to keep to themselves and not act out, or be helpful to others. The people are artistic and expressive; this expressiveness is not like the "Emo" cry for help. The "Emo" cry for help is more of an artistic add-something-to-the-world expressiveness. In this way, unlike their "Emo" counterparts, they provide something to their fans.

By contrast, the "Emo" musician plays a song that cries out for pity. The pre-teens who fill this category are often those who are seeking acceptance into any group, and the overly depressive music appeals to them. This does not provide a creative outlet for them, but rather takes from them at the core of their being. They cannot add to the world around them when they are being robbed of who they are.

Looking around the web, you find some sites that will tell you "Emo" is in its third cycle; the first coming in the 1980's, then again in the 1990's, with the most recent cycle coming up within the last couple of years. Artists who fall into this group include Fall Out Boy, Panic! At the Disco, and Cute Is What We Aim For. This rollercoaster cycle of use for "Emo" music is like a manic depressive person. The record labels think they can make money off it, they push it out onto the shelves, and when they cannot, it goes back into the background.

Fashion of the "Goth" and "Emo"

While there are many similarities and differences between the groups, one of the most important is the area of how they dress. From the clothes the wear to how they style their hair, the looks for the "Goth" and "Emo" are what set them apart visually. While both groups wear black clothes, dark makeup, and assorted fashion accessories, a "Goth" will not wear Converse.

The greatest influence of the base style of "Goth" comes out of the 18th century. Certain aspects are traced to Victorian dress. Some have tried to establish a link to the world of extreme sexual fetishism and the darker side of human sexual nature, given the use of leather, rubber, and latex at times to cause the turning of heads. While there may be some fact to this type of statement, the limit of research undertaken did not delve into that area of human habit. Even with the style of dress there is an influence on society seen in many formats.

In many movies, such as those with vampire-themed overtones, "Goth" dress is prevalent throughout. Most times the look is mainly Victorian, due to established forms of thinking by the public at large. As an example: in the movie *Underworld* (2003) the heroine wears all leather with a corset as one of the most defining features once the long leather trench coat comes off. In other movies, Gothic dress comes in many colors. The colors used fit in with the time period being depicted; such is the case in *Interview with a Vampire* (1994).

Each movie in which "Goth" fashion is portrayed adds an element of exposure to popular culture, and develops an even further blurring of the lines. Another example would come from the movie *The Matrix* (1999), in which our heroes go around in dark clothing and trench coats meant to set them apart from the other "sheep."

The new trend in popular culture is the "Emo" style of fashion, which takes from many different groups in society. What they take from the "Goth" is dark clothing and makeup. The subtle differences are the tightness of clothing and how hair is styled to cover half of the face. Add in the use of clothing styles used by skaters and punks and you are left with a formula for getting lost in the crowd. This does not add substance to your life; rather, it takes it away and leaves you searching for your place in life.

The "Emo" fashion is stated as being very open and expressive in nature. The use of tight clothing appears as a must, from tee shirts to jeans. Another element of the style is listed as a hooded sweater, and even the layered look with a short sleeved shirt over a long sleeved is another example. Seemingly, all parts of the fashion are taken from other groups. The layers portion of the look can just as easily be associated with the grunge look from the early 1990's. As for the hooded sweaters, they are part of the skater look or even street gangs.

Cultural Interactions

Through the examination of the "Goth" in society, the unity and groupthink of the "Goths" is what sustains the group's importance in society. Considering the second definition of "substantive", the findings in the previous research contradict the ideas of having independence. Simultaneously, it is hard to say that "Emo" subculture has a sufficient backbone to support itself, either. The "Goth" culture can be compared to the Transcendental movement; both share the common hatred for society, yet both groups exist primarily because of their relationship counterpart to society.

Although previous research proves the gothic community to be dependent within as well as on society, for its purpose, it seems gothic individuals' original intent is self-sufficiency, as individuality is highly regarded and prized within the community. Another example of this contradiction of individuality is exemplified on for "Goth" created by "Goth" web community sites. On the site Goth.net, Preston Eider (2001) provides a complete layout of how to be "Goth" for those who want in, but don't know how.

The level of how each culture interacts within their group and others can be hard to determine. Most people agree the "Emo" movement is mostly teens, and possibly some in their twenties. The claim is laid out to be about creative artistic expression through music. Websites abound that lay out the road map to becoming "Emo". How you should dress, behave, and the music you are listening to are listed for you. They also work to dispel the association between them and those who harm themselves.

The level of depression a person who is part of this culture deals with varies, but a way to build a higher acceptance level is rumored to be through cutting. The counter argument is that this type of behavior is not encouraged, and those who do are severely disturbed on a psychological level. Why then would so many others use this as a way to acceptance if it was highly discouraged? The attempt to present this image to the public is weak at its core, and an attempt to keep the public docile allowing control of the weaker minded among them.

Not all who are "Emo" act in this manner. Many can participate in music, fashion, and culture without the self-destructive behaviors. These are the people who are not in the forefront of the culture. They do not lead the others; rather they sit on the side and wait until they feel the need to speak out and attempt to dispel the notion about cutting and the "Emo." Even as the new reports hit the airwaves and the printing presses, the lack of good things being said about "Emos" is a drain on the group which calls out that attention be given to them. This is not the path to individuality, but rather a cycle that will lead to a dependence on others. The dependence, in turn, will drain the people around them and cause a collapse in society, much like problems that are felt in the helping professions when attempting to provide care for those with mental and emotional problems best served by the institutions of olden days.

After a side by side comparison of the groups, the "Goth" life-style would be more substantive to a person. Given the way the members of the community interact with each other, and lend their support is almost enough of a reason in its own right. The "Emo" lifestyle is embedded with thoughts and behaviors that are harmful in nature to a person on many levels. After a Devils Lake, North Dakota news story about the "Emo" subculture hit the airwaves in 2007, the "Emo" response was clear and apparent in many "blog" responses filled with poorly written sentences and words chosen that were more expletive in nature than anything else, as read on *So More Scene* (2007).

Multiple sites that feature this news story exist; they get mostly the same crowd around them. These individuals use their limited education in a vain attempt to draw attention to themselves, some even admitting to partaking in the harmful behaviors mentioned. This provides yet even more examples of how the "Emo" culture takes away from its members without giving anything back. The outlook on the "Emo" culture had prompted the Russian government to call for a ban on certain aspects of the culture, mainly those who promote harm to the person such as self mutilation or suicide.

The "Goth" will continue to challenge everything you believe in. They want people to not only believe in an idea or and ideal, but know why they feel that way. Blind acceptance can lead a society down a path of destruction and end with its ruin; it could be political, economical, or social. Given the current state of the world as a whole, maybe we all need to be more "Goth."

References

Adler, G. (Producer), & Malone, W. (Director). *House on haunted hill* [Motion Picture]. United States: Dark Castle Entertainment.

Baumeister, R. (1997). *Evil: Inside human violence and cruelty.* New York: Henry Holt and Company.

Benech-Lui, P. (2008). Modern gothic. *Ornament, 32,* 38-41.

Bernacchi, R. (Producer), & Wiseman, L. (Director). *Underworld* [Motion Picture]. United States: Lakeshore Entertainment.

Brill, D. (2008). *Goth culture: Gender, sexuality, and style.* Oxford: Berg.

Burk, Lorelei. (n.d.) Rose Mortem: Dark and Romantic Finery. *Gothic Beauty.* 50-52.

Carlson, P. (2007, January, 23). A piercing look at goth culture and fashion. [Electronic Version]. *The Washington Post*, p. Co1.

Critchell, Samantha. (2008, October 1). Fashion Visits the Dark Side in Gothic Exhibit. The Associated Press, [Electronic Version].

Dark independent. (2008). Retrieved from the Web February 17, 2009. http://www.darkindependent.net

Dullum, T. (Producer). (2009). *News broadcast.* [Television Series]. Grand Folks: WDAZ News.

Eider, P. (2001). What is goth? Retrieved from the Web January 28, 2009. http://www.goth.net

Emo corner: The emo hangout. (2008). Retrieved from the Web January 28, 2009. http://www.emo-corner.com

Farkas, C. (2006). *Contemporary gothic.* London: Reaktion Books.

Geffen, D. (Producer), & Jordan, N. (Director). *Interview with the vampire* [Motion Picture]. United States: Geffen Pictures.

Guardian, The. (2008). Retrieved from the Web March 3, 2009. http://www.guardian.co.uk/music/2008/jul/22/ruussian.emo

Hodkinson, P. (2002) *Goth: Identity, style, and subculture.* Oxford: Berg.

Lindberg, Christine A. (Ed.). (2002). *The Oxford American college dictionary.* (2nd ed.). New York: Penguin Putnam Inc.

Luv Emo: What is emo? (2007). Retrieved from the Web February 14, 2009. http://www.luv- emo.com

Myerson, J. (2000). *Transcendentalism: A reader.* Oxford: Oxford University Press.

Popkin, H. (2006). What exactly is 'emo,' anyway? Retrieved from the Web February 24, 2009. http://www.msnbc.msn.com

Robinson, C. (2008). The goth culture: Its history, stereotype, religious aspects, etc. Retrieved from the Web February 14, 2009. http://www.religioustolerance.org

Rutledge, C. (2008). Vulnerable goth teens: The role of schools in this psychosocial high-risk culture. *Journal of School Health, 78.*

Sands, Sarah. (2006, August 16). Emo cult warning for parents. Associated Newspapers Ltd. [Electronic Version].

So More Scene. (2007). Retrieved from the Web March 3, 2009. http://www.somorescene.com/2007/02/28/news-flash-dangerous-emo-trend-might-take-hold-of-your-impressionable-teen/

Spooner, Catherine. (2004). *Fashion: Gothic bodies.* Manchester: Manchester University Press.

Wachowski, A. (Producer), & Wachowski, L. (Director). *The matrix* [Motion Picture]. United States: Warner Bros.

Wittaker, J. (2007). Dark webs: Goth subcultures in cyber space. [Electronic Version]. *Gothic Studies, 9,* 35-45.

Disabling Misconceptions:
A study on the dating practices of physically disabled women and
able-bodied men

Christie Laneve
English 102
Dr. Jeremy Sideris
April 30, 2008

Abstract

Physically disabled women are not given the same opportunities in dating as able-bodied women. This study was an effort to explore why this occurs, and whether it has more to do with the women's physical limitations or the misconceptions able-bodied men have regarding their capabilities. To discover the answer, 10 physically disabled women and 10 able-bodied men from Edinboro University of Pennsylvania were each surveyed. Results from these surveys indicated the dating practices of physically disabled women and able-bodied men are impacted more by the mistreatments and misconceptions of the men than the women's actual physical limitations. However, these results could have been affected due to the fact that surveys were only distributed to students at Edinboro University, a campus well-known for its significant disabled population. Since the able-bodied men surveyed are more likely to see, meet, and talk to physically disabled women while on this campus, the misconceptions referred to in the literature may not be as evident in the survey results from this study.

Disabling Misconceptions:
A study on the dating practices of physically disabled women and
able-bodied men

My initial motivation to explore the dating practices of physically disabled women came out of an interview I did with a physically
disabled woman at Edinboro University. She was disabled by a car
accident, and is now paralyzed from the waist down. We discussed
many aspects of her life, and how becoming disabled has impacted
her. When asked whether she has dated anyone since the accident,

> M. Gill (personal communication, February 12, 2008) stated
> "I've been out on like three dates, but it's still very weird. I
> spent so much time dating before. It's a very different scene
> now. When someone wants to date me...I'm like what's the
> matter with you?...you can't see what's the matter with me. But
> I didn't have that comfort level that I had before...I wasn't my-
> self. It's kind of a different way to do it now."

Her response intrigued me, and I found myself wanting to learn
more about the reasoning behind her current views on dating. As a
result, when it came time to pick a topic for my study, I decided this
was the perfect opportunity to further explore the dating practices
of physically disabled women.

When you do not encounter a certain subculture often, it is easy
to overlook its complexity. The world of physically disabled women is
one such group which tends to be disregarded or judged prematurely
by the able-bodied, in particular, men. Able-bodied is a term used
to describe those who are "physically fit and healthy" and capable
of walking without any assistance (Soanes, 2005, p. 2). The misconceptions able-bodied men have can affect their willingness to date a
woman with a physical disability. According to the literature, these
men often have preconceived ideas concerning the women's sexuality, self esteem, and the ability to have children, which are, in many
ways, accurate. These misconceptions can have terrible consequenc-
es, such as the mistreatment of physically disabled women in the form
of partner abuse. Subsequently, the dating practices of physically dis-

abled women and able-bodied men are impacted more by the mistreatments and misconceptions of the men than the women's actual
physical limitations.

My goal in conducting this study was to enlighten able-bodied
men about the truths behind their misconceptions concerning physically disabled women. By doing this, it will give men a chance to see
those aspects which exist in all women, regardless of their physical
appearance or functional limitations. It will allow the men to better understand and relate to a subculture which is, in fact, much like
our own, just with some modifications. As a result, it is my hope that
more physically disabled women will attain the romantic relationships with able-bodied men they so desire.

Some men may resist me out of the idea they are not part of
the problem, that it is more of the women's shortcomings which affects their ability to date able-bodied men. Other men may feel I am
attacking the male population in general for having discriminatory
views. However, it is not the intent of this study to attack one group
by placing blame on an entire population based on the conduct of a
select number. I hope able-bodied men will not take this study as a
personal attack on their character, but rather look at it with an open
mind and see it as an opportunity to broaden their views.

I must admit I may not be completely objective when it comes to
the issue of physically disabled women having the same opportunities
in dating as able-bodied women. Since coming to Edinboro University, I have made many friends who are physically disabled. Through
our discussions, I have learned of their struggles to be accepted and
treated like everyone else, especially when it comes to dating. As a result, my ability to stay impartial on the subject matter may have been
influenced somewhat during the course of my research.

Seeing as many of my friends are part of the group I was studying, I felt the need to give them the respect they deserved in this paper. Subsequently, I chose to refer to my female population as physically disabled, rather than handicapped. The reason for this lies in
the definition of the latter, which simply used to mean "a physical,
mental, or emotional condition that interferes with a person's normal functioning" (Stegman, 2005, p. 637). However, this word is now

seen by many as derogatory, and meaning "an individual or group of individuals at a disadvantage" (VandenBos, 2007, p. 428). This implies that having a disability somehow makes one weak and less of a person. This is simply not true. Just because a person's physical state is not optimal, does not mean he or she is a weak person or means any less in this world.

Literature Review

Mistreatments & Misconceptions

Dating is something which can be seen as a challenge for any woman; however, women with physical disabilities must face a layer of issues able-bodies women do not (Wiegenink, 2006). Unfortunately, "stigmatizing attitudes toward people with disabilities are still prevalent in our society" (Miller, 1999, p. xvii).

Sexual Intimacy

There are many societal misconceptions regarding the sexuality of physically disabled women which have an impact in their ability to form and maintain romantic relationships with able-bodied men. Many of these negative views are portrayed by the media, which depicts them as either being "overly capable lovers focusing all attention onto their partner and not acknowledging their own sexual desires" or as sad, bitter people who are somehow damaged (Mona, n.d.; ¶ 4). Due to these representations, as well as a general lack of knowledge by the public, many able-bodied men have a distorted view concerning the sexuality of physically disabled women.

The most prevalent belief about the sexuality of physically disabled women focuses on the idea that they are unable to have sex (Aryault, 1981, Howland, 2001, Jaeger, 2005, Marinelli, 1984). Seeing as sexual compatibility is a pertinent issue for many when deciding whom to date, some able-bodied men are deterred from asking out a woman whom they believe is unable to fill that critical need (Kroll, 1992). Another misconception which some able-bodied men have relates to the idea that physically disabled women are "especially good sexually" (Howland, 2001, p. 62). Subsequently, they will seek these women out in an effort to act out some sort of fetish (Howland, 2001). These distorted views of physically disabled women often lead to the unfortunate reality of partner abuse.

Abuse

According to Copal (2006), "The Center for Research on Women with Disabilities published research findings which indicated that abuse is a major problem for women with disabilities" (p. 114). They suffer more from partner abuse than able-bodied women due to social and emotional factors related specifically to their disability as well as negative societal perceptions (Copal, 2006).

While a lack of social skills and low self esteem are issues which can impede dating for any woman, sources indicate they are especially damaging for women with physical disabilities. Women who have congenital physical disabilities often lack the foundation of key social and emotional skills due to increased parental overprotection during critical development periods. The reason for this lays in the fact that many parents shelter physically disabled children from engaging in developmentally appropriate activities out of fear that he or she will get emotionally hurt. (Howland, 2001). This can result in "lower happiness, self esteem, perceived popularity, and self-consciousness, and higher levels of anxiety, all factors which can interfere with successful social interactions..." (Howland, 2001, p. 44). For women who developed their physical disability later in life, dealing with reevaluating how they socialize can be a heavy burden, which can easily become frustrating. Their previous techniques of attracting a partner, such as the swinging of hips when walking, may no longer be plausible, and many get discouraged and become less social due to this fact (Mona, n.d.).

With their emotional and social defenses lowered (Nosek, 2001), physically disabled women are subject to getting and staying in abusive relationships more frequently. They are more likely to trust able-bodied men in situations which would have otherwise raised flags for able-bodied women with more dating experience and confidence (Howland, 2001). In addition, fears of being rejected, when combined with a "strong desire to be partnered" (Hassouneh-Phillips, 2005, p. 227), also contribute to a physically disabled woman's increased vulnerability towards dating "men who always have to be the one in control" (Howland, 2001, p. 57). This domineering characteristic is often a sign of a future abuser.

Those who abuse physically disabled women frequently have misconceptions regarding the women's worth. Some believe the societal view that physically disabled women are "damaged goods who can neither attract, nor are they worthy of the attention of a quality partner" (Howland, 2001, p. 41). Subsequently, abusive men think they can easily control and take advantage of these women because they are so desperate for companionship they would be less likely to leave, no matter how bad the mistreatment (Howland, 2001).

Having Children

Physically disabled women are often seen by able-bodied men as unable to have children (Howland, 2001). For some men, having a women whom they view as intact and able to reproduce is a necessity, and as a result, they will write off a woman who is physically disabled before even finding out if she is actually capable of becoming pregnant. For those whom understand that many physically disabled women can in fact become pregnant, other societal issues come into play. Not only do women with physical disabilities have to deal with their own doubts and fears concerning pregnancy, but those of others as well. There is an inherent fear amongst those in society that disabilities are inherited, and subsequently, women who have physical disabilities should not be allows to bring children into the world who may also be disabled (Browne, 1985).

Physical Limitations

Accessibility

While able-bodied women can be spontaneous and "pick up and go at a moment's notice," those with physical disabilities are forced to plan ahead to ensure there will be no accessibility issues wherever they go. Making sure there are elevators, wheelchair accessible restrooms, and adequate seating space are just some of the accessibility concerns physically disabled women have to deal with when looking to go out on a date. In addition, transportation also becomes an issue for physically disabled women. Unlike able-bodied women, those with physical disabilities must often rely on others to get where they want to be, especially if they cannot afford a modified vehicle. While the functional challenges the physically disabled must face in order to go out on a date are not impossible, having to deal with them everyday can be an exhausting ordeal for all those involved (Love, n.d.).

Sexual Intimacy

"Every person, regardless of gender, age, or disability, is a sexual being" (Kroll, 1992, p.33). A woman's physical state has no bearing on her desire for the same emotional "closeness, affection, and sexual stimulation" as able-bodied women (Love, n.d., ¶ 30). Most women who are physically disabled are capable of sexual satisfaction in some way despite their physical limitations. Depending upon the nature of a physical disability, "sexual functioning is affected to varying degrees" (Mona, n.d., ¶ 22). Subsequently, certain modifications are often required, such as "changing the timing of sexual intimacy, positions, type of sexual activities, means of contraception, and the nature of communication surrounding sexual activities" (Kroll, 1992, p. 42).

Women with congenital disabilities have grown up knowing their bodies a certain way and subsequently have had more time to develop their sexual self. However, for women who acquired their disability later in life, they must face entirely different challenges when it comes to the issue of sexual intimacy. Many women with onset physical disabilities had already developed their sexual identity before becoming physically disabled. Consequently, they must learn to let go of their former sexual self and redefine who they are sexually, a task which can be frustrating and time consuming (Mona, n.d.).

Having Children

"Physically, many women with disabilities are capable of conceiving and bearing children" (Krill, 1992, p. 68). In fact, many women with physical disabilities frequently have unwanted pregnancies due to the fact that fertility is usually "unaffected by the disability and most methods of birth control pose unique dangers for disabled women..." (Deloach, 1981, p. 80). For instance, the pill, which is one of the most effective forms of contraception, is especially dangerous for those who are paralyzed due to its tendency to produce blood clots. Subsequently, many women with physical disabilities must rely on less effective methods of birth control which pose less of a threat to their health, such as contraceptive foam (Deloach, 1981).

Another issue women with physical disabilities must face when it comes to having children is whether their children could contract the same disability. In fact, most disabilities are not genetic, and many who have been disabled since birth attained their disability as a result of other factors, such as extremely low birth weight. For those who do have disabilities which could be genetically passed on, they must make the decision as to whether having a child is right for them (Kroll, 1992). In the end, those with disabilities "have the right to have or not to have children, and ultimately their choice must be completely theirs" (Kroll, 1992, p. 68).

Methods

Fifteen physically disabled women and fifteen able-bodied men were the subjects of this study. Those who participated were students at Edinboro University, ranged in age from eighteen to twenty-nine, and were either African American or Caucasian. In addition, those involved in the study also ranged in political affiliation from none, to liberal/Democrat, to moderate, to conservative/Republican. Finally, exclusive to women with physical disabilities, the onset of their disability was asked, in particular, whether they were born with their condition. These demographic questions were asked in an effort to see if certain subgroups would be formed.

The primary research for this study was conducted through surveys distributed to students at Edinboro University. In regard to the Likert questions, there were twelve on the men's and twelve on the women's.

Likert questions

The basis behind question one on the women's survey was to corroborate facts stating many women with physical disabilities are overprotected by their parents. In contrast, question ten on the men's survey was meant to find out if men prefer dating women who are independent of their parents.

The seconds question on the women's survey was intended to find whether the women had proper social skills. In contrast, question six on the men's survey was meant to discover if able-bodied men see physically disabled women as being active in social settings, which would confirm or deny if physically disabled women lack self confidence and social skills.

The reasoning behind question three was to find whether physically disabled women feel able-bodied men pity them. In contrast, question twelve on the men's survey was meant to find out if the men actually do pity physically disabled women.

The fourth, seventh, and eleventh questions were to find out how the women value sexual intimacy, and how their disability affects this area. In contrast, questions four, eight, and eleven in the men's survey were meant to find out how much the men valued sexual intimacy, and if they would want to be intimate with a woman who had a physical disability.

Question five on the women's survey was intended to find whether physically disabled women think able-bodied men stereotype them. The sixth question on the women's survey was to determine whether physically disabled women want to get married and have children. In contrast, question two on the men's survey was meant to find if able-bodied men think physically disabled women are capable of having biological children.

Question eight on the women's survey was meant to find whether the women thought the media played a role in able-bodied men stereotyping them, In contrast, question nine on the men's survey was meant to see whether the men thought society portrayed women with physical disabilities in a negative light.

The ninth question on the women's survey, and the first and fifth questions on the men's, were intended to show the association between how physically disabled women view themselves and how able-bodied men, in turn, view them.

The tenth question on the women's survey was meant to find if the women with physical disabilities prefer dating able-bodied men. In contrast, question seven on the men's survey was intended to find whether an able-bodied man would date a woman with a physical disability.

The twelfth question was meant to discover whether women with physical disabilities are more desperate to be in a relationship than able-bodied women. In contrast, question three on the men's survey was meant to determine whether able-bodied men prefer being the dominant personality in the relationship.

Open-ended questions

There were seven open-ended questions on the women's survey and five on the men's survey. Question one on the women's survey was intended to find if physically disabled women felt able-bodied men judge them based on their disability. Conversely, question one on the men's survey was meant to find if men tend to focus on the physical challenges related to dating a physically disabled woman.

Question two on the women's survey was meant to evaluate additional functional challenges women with physical disabilities must face when it comes to dating. Question three on the women's survey was meant to find if any of the women had suffered from abuse by an able-bodied partner. In contrast, question three on the men's survey was meant to find whether able-bodied men view women with physical disabilities as desperate to be in a relationship.

Question four on the women's survey was a fun question meant to lighten the mood after the previous question on abuse. The fifth question on the women's survey was intended to determine the level of dependence women with physical disabilities have on their partners. The sixth question on the women's survey was meant to find whether the women's physical disability had an impact on past relationships, and in what ways. Question seven on the women's survey was intended to give the women an opportunity to inform able-bodied men of things they might otherwise not be comfortable bringing up in person.

The second question on the men's survey was intended to find whether peer pressure would impact an able-bodied man's willingness to date a woman with a physical disability. Question four on the men's survey was meant to get a general idea of what able-bodied men thought of when presented with the idea of physically disabled women dating. The fifth and final question on the men's survey was intended to find whether an able-bodied man would date a woman with a physical disability and the reasoning behind their views.

The participants in this study were selected in various ways. In regard to the men's surveys, a few were distributed to men in Scranton Residence Hall. However, the need for efficiency led to the abandonment of this tactic. Subsequently, the rest were given to two professors who distributed them to their classes. The women's surveys were distributed on the first floor of Scranton Residence Hall, which is part of the dormitory reserved for students with disabilities requiring personal care (PC). They were passed out door to door, but it was not known whether the women would care to participate in this study. The personal care assistants were asked if they would be willing to assist those who could not complete the form on their own. Some women filled them out shortly after they were distributed, and their surveys were collected that same night. For the other women who said they would fill out a survey later, permission was given to have the surveys left in the personal care room to be picked up at another time.

Results

Women's Survey

- The following paragraph will focus on the majority results from the distributed surveys.

Question one stated "my parents are overprotective," and showed 60% of women disagreed to some extent with this statement. For the second question, results showed 70% of the women agreed they feel confident in social situations. In regard to question three, which said "able-bodied men just feel sorry for me," 50% of women surveyed did not agree with this statement. Results from question four indicated 80% of the women agreed that sexual intimacy is important to them. Question five showed 90% of the women feel people stereotype them based on their disability. According to question six, 80% of the women can see themselves getting married and having children. Results from question seven showed 60% of the women feel their sexuality is affected by their physical limitations. In regard to the eighth question, 80% of women stated they feel the media affects outside perceptions related to how physically disabled women date. The ninth question, which stated "I feel physically attractive," showed 80% of women agreed with this statement. Results from question ten showed 60% of the women prefer dating someone who is also physically disabled. Question eleven said "I consider myself to be sexually experienced," and results showed 40% of women agreed, 40% disagreed, and 10% had no opinion on the subject. The twelfth question, which stated "I am always looking for a romantic relationship," did not show a clear majority, with 50% agreeing and 50% disagreeing.

Men's Survey

~ The following paragraph will focus on the majority results from the distributed surveys.

Question one, which stated "when looking to date someone, physical appearance is important to me," showed 90% of men agreed with this statement. "Physically disabled women can have biological children" was the second question, and results showed 60% of men agreed with this statement. In regard to question three, 90% of men had no opinion as to whether they prefer being the dominant personality in a relationship. Results from question four showed 60% of men disagreed with the statement "sexual intimacy with a physically disabled woman would be just as fulfilling as with a women who was able-bodied." Furthermore, the fifth question showed 40% of men feel having a trophy wife would be ideal. "I frequently see physically disabled women in social settings" was the sixth question, and results showed 70% of men feel this statement accurate. Results from question seven showed 40% of men would date someone who has a physical disability and 40% had no opinion on the subject. In regard to the eighth question, 90% of men said sexual intimacy is important to them. "I prefer dating independent women" was the tenth question, and survey results showed 90% of men agreed with this statement. Survey results from question twelve showed 50% of men feel sorry for a physically disabled woman when they see her.

Discussion

My initial beliefs concerning the dating practices of physically disabled women and able-bodied men were, in many ways, substantiated by the data I collected from my study; however, it must be made clear that certain aspects of my argument were negated by what I found.

According to literature on the subject, as well as data collected from my surveys, able-bodied men lack knowledge and/or possess certain misconceptions about physically disabled women and the aspects related to their romantic relationships. When surveyed, 60% of women stated they prefer dating able-bodied men. However, with only 40% of the men surveyed stating they would date a women with a physical disability, it is clear why many physically disabled women have difficulty forming the relationships they so desire.

We live in a society which places so much value on outward appearance and the idea of "normalcy," that women who somehow look different, or do not fit the ideal standard presented by the media, are often overlooked (Kroll, 1992). For women with physical disabilities, this is a difficult stigma to overcome. Even though a majority of the women surveyed feel physically attractive, women with physical disabilities are frequently confused by society's ideas concerning sexiness, and subsequently, many do not know if they are considered sexually desirable by able-bodied men (Mona, n.d.). This stigma surrounding the physical appearance further established by the fact that 30% of able-bodied men surveyed stated physical attraction as being a reason why they would not date a physically disabled woman. For instance, one participant stated "I don't find it attractive; it's not that I dislike disabled women, I just wouldn't date one."

Able-bodied men can also be impacted by how other people view physically disabled women. For instance, "advice or pressure from friends or family may discourage dating, particularly if the partner's friends look down on dating a woman with a disability" (Howland, 2001, p. 51). When asked if peer pressure would affect their willingness to date a physically disabled women, a majority of the men said no, stating reasons such as: "I run my own life," "if I'm comfortable that's what matters," and "I don't usually listen to the crowd." In hindsight, the question asked was rather leading, and some of the men may have not been able to admit how much the views of others can impact their own action. This may account for the anomaly between what the literature states about the issue and what the surveys revealed.

In addition to the issues surrounding physical appearance, results from the distributed surveys reinforced literature stating able-bodied men have a lack of knowledge, as well as certain stereotypical beliefs regarding the sexual capabilities of physically disabled women.

For instance, when asked whether physically disabled women were sexually inexperienced, 70% of men had no opinion on the subject. This shows able-bodied men either disregard, or do not think about the idea of physically disabled women being sexually intimate. This lack of understanding can produce misconceptions, such as the idea that women are somehow damaged and "can't have sex, don't want sex, or are not interested in sex" (Kroll, 1992, p. 16). This idea was further established by one of the women surveyed, who stated "...able-bodied men look at me and think wow she can't do anything sexual and move on."

For the men who are aware that most physically disabled women are capable of sexual intimacy, another issue comes to light. When asked whether sexual intimacy with a physically disabled woman would be as fulfilling as with an able-bodied woman, a majority said it would not. This indicated able-bodied men feel a woman's disability would negatively impact sexual intimacy. In addition, with 90% of men surveyed stating sexual intimacy is important to them, it is evident why able-bodied men often disregard physically disabled women as a romantic possibility.

In reality, most women with physical disabilities are capable of having fully gratifying sexual relationships (Kroll, 1992). In fact 80% of women surveyed said sexual intimacy was important to them, and an additional 40% considered themselves to be sexually experienced. However, certain modifications are often necessary to accommodate their physical limitations, such as changing the positions and level of communication involved (Kroll, 1992). When surveyed, over half the women stated their sexuality is affected in some way by their physical limitations. However, this fact does not mean that having sex with a physically disabled woman cannot be just as emotionally and physically satisfying as with an able-bodied woman.

Misconceptions concerning the sexuality of physically disabled women can lead to their mistreatment by able-bodied men. Some men who have sexual dysfunction issues or a lack of sexual interest may seek out physically disabled women out of the idea that they are unable to have sex (Howland, 2001). Conversely, some men may purposefully seek out disabled women due to the belief they have learned to cope by becoming great at oral sex (Love, n.d.). These misconceptions concerning the women's sexuality can lead to them being taken advantage of by able-bodied men.

Another factor which can attribute to physically disabled women being abused is that some of the women have poor self esteem and social skills as a result of their disability. For those born with their disability, this is frequently caused by parental overprotection (Howland, 2001). However, survey results showed over half the women did not feel their parents were overprotective. This anomaly could be due to the fact that not all parents of disabled children are any more overprotective that the parents of able-bodied children. For those who attained their disability later in life, social and self esteem can be a result of having to reevaluate who they are and how others now view them (Mona, n.d.). As a result of their lower social and emotional skills, controlling men can seek out physically disabled women due to the idea that they are weak and desperate to be in a relationship (Howland, 2001). Further substantiating this idea is the fact that 30% of men surveyed stated they prefer being the dominant personality in a relationship, which is a common characteristic of an abuser. In addition, half of the men stated they feel sorry for physically disabled women, and half of the women stated they are always looking for a romantic relationship. These results showed the women are looking for relationships and the men pity them because of their physical state, a paradigm which can lead to the able-bodied men taking advantage of physically disabled women. When asked whether they have ever been mistreated in a romantic relationship, 1 out of 10 women surveyed said she had been a victim of both verbal and sexual abuse.

While some physically disabled women have poor social and emotional skills, results from distributed surveys indicated 70% of the women feel confident in social situations. In comparison, 70% of men surveyed stated they see physically disabled women in social settings. This shows not all women with physical disabilities are shy and lack adequate self esteem. Many are just as outgoing and socially present as able-bodied women.

According to literature, some men have the misconception that physically disabled women are unable to have their own biological children (Howland, 2001). Many men hold the ideals of the evolutionary theory, which emphasizes the importance of being able to reproduce and further your heredity (Myers, 2008). Given this fact, it is not surprising that 40% of men surveyed stated they would prefer to have a "trophy wife." For instance, when asked whether physically disabled women have more obstacles in dating, one man answered "Yes due to the fact they are disabled. It goes against nature in a way. The strong survive." As is shown by this quote, physically disabled women are seen as damaged, and are written off by many able-bodied men who are uncomfortable finding out whether their way of thinking is even accurate. In contrast, 60% of the men surveyed stated that physically disabled women are able to have biological children. The difference in what the literature states and what was attained from my survey can be attributed to the format of the question. Had it been presented as an open-ended question where the men had to give the reasoning behind their answer, results more consistent with the literature may have been seen.

Most physically disabled women are, in fact, capable of having their own children because fertility is rarely affected by a disability. When surveyed, 80% of the women stated they want to get married and have children someday. However, other misconceptions men have could hinder this dream. Some men make the false assumption that the women would pass on their disability to their children (Kroll, 1992). In reality, most physical disabilities are not genetic, and are often attained for other reason, such as low birth weight. Another concern able-bodied men can have relates to how well the woman would be able to care for the child given her functional limitations. Some men feel they would end up not only having to help care for the woman, but would also be solely responsible for the care of the child. While some women may need assistance depending on the degree of disability, many are capable of raising children and should be given the same opportunity as any other woman to have a child (Kroll, 1992).

As can be inferred from the previous paragraphs, the dating practices of physically disabled women and able-bodied men are impacted more by the mistreatments and misconceptions of the men than the women's actual physical limitations. Many physically disabled women are capable of engaging in the same activities as able-bodied women, but just in a slightly different way. In the technologically advanced world we live in, there are ways of working around the women's physical limitations. However, the distorted views some able-bodied men have of these women can stop a relationship before it even has a chance to start, or even worse, lead to the women's abuse.

My study is unique because it focuses specifically on the relationship between physically disabled women and able-bodied men. Many sources I came across during my secondary research gave a broad view of how the disabled date, and did not focus directly on this relationship. I wanted to focus on the interaction between physically disabled women and able-bodied men because of the emotional aspects unique to men and women; women tend to characteristically have this desire for closeness and affection, while men are often afraid of commitment. It is this very dynamic which can cause issues for any woman who wants to date a man. However, when you look at an able-bodied man dating a physically disabled woman, a whole other layer of challenges unique to that relationship become evident.

While my study did effectively substantiate my thesis, there were some limitations involved which could have impacted my findings. In regard to the secondary research, there were not many resources on the subject of the physically disabled dating, and even fewer focusing on women in particular. However, one of the reasons I chose this topic was because not much is known concerning it. I wanted to shed light on an issue which is not frequently discussed. In addition, another factor which could have impacted my results is the fact that I distributed my surveys to students as Edinboro University, a campus well-known for its significant disabled population. Since able-bodied students are more likely to see, meet, and talk to physically disabled women while on this campus, the misconceptions referred to in the literature may not be as evident in my survey results. In addition, the sensitive subject matter
contained in my surveys may have impacted my total population because I received only about half of the surveys I actually distributed to physically disabled women. A larger population would

have been ideal so my results would be even more valid. However, I am content with the number I received given this is a subject many are not used to, nor comfortable discussing. It is my hope that others will read this study and want to continue researching the dynamic relationships of physically disabled women and able-bodied men. If more people take this information and explore it further, then more knowledge will be available which can have a positive impact on the population. If the data I have collected helps even one able-bodied man give a physically disabled woman a chance, when he would have otherwise not, then I feel my study was a success.

References

Ayrault, E.W. (1981). *Sex, love, and the physically handicapped*. New York: Continuum Publishing Company.

Browne, S.E., Connors, D., & Stern, N. (1985). *With the power of each breath: A disabled woman's anthology*. Pittsburgh: Cleis Press.

Copal, L.C. (2006). Partner abuse in the physically disabled women. [Electronic Version]. *Perspectives in Psychiatric Care, 41*, 114-129.

Deloach, C., & Greer, B.G. (1981). *Adjustment to severe physical disability: A metamorphosis*. New York: McGraw-Hill Book Company.

Hassouneh-Philips, D. & McNeff, E. (2005). "I thought I was less worthy: Low sexual and body esteem and increased vulnerability to intimate partner abuse in women with physical disabilities [Electronic Version]. *Sexuality and Disability, 23*, 227-240.

Howland, C. & Rintala, D.H. (2001). Dating behaviors of women with physical disabilities. [Electronic Version]. *Sexuality and Disability, 19*, 41-67.

Jaeger, P., & Bowman, C.A. (2005). *Understanding disability*. Westport, Connecticut: Praeger Publishers.

Kroll, K., & Klein, E.L. (1992). Enabling romance: *A guide to love, sex, and relationships for the disabled*. New York: Harmony Books.

Love, T. (n.d.). How to meet, date, and "do it" when you're disabled. Retrieved from the Web February 26, 2008. http://www.mypleasure.com/education/sexed/how_to_when_youre_ disabled.asp

Marinelli, R.P., & Dell Orto, A.E. (1984). *The psychological & social impact of physical disability*. New York: Springer Publishing Company.

Miller, N.B., & Sammons, C.C. (1999). *Everybody's different*. Baltimore, Maryland: Paul H. Brookes Publishing Co.

Mona, L. (n.d.). Sexuality & disability. Retrieved from the Web February 26, 2008. http://www.mypleasure.com/education/sexed/sex_and_disability_history_and_practices. asp

Myers, D.G. (2008). *Exploring psychology.* New York: Worth Publishers.

Nosek, M.A., Foley, C.C., Hughes, R.B., & Howland, C.A. (2001). Vulnerability for the abuse among women with disabilities. [Electronic Version]. *Sexuality and disability, 19,* 177-189.

Soanes, C. (Ed.). (2005). *Pocket Oxford English dictionary.* (10th ed.). New York: Oxford University Press Inc.

Stegman, J.K. (2005). *Stedman's medical dictionary for the health professions and nursing.* (5th Ed.). Baltimore: Lippicott and Wilkins.

VandenBos, G.R. (Ed.). (2007) *APA dictionary of psychology.* (1st ed.). Washington DC: American Psychological Association.

Weigenink, D. J. H. G., Roebroeck, M.E., Donkervoort, M., Stam, H. J., & Cohen-Kettenis, P. T. (2006). Social and sexual relationships of adolescents and young adults with Cerebral palsy: A review. [Electronic Version]. *Clinical Rehabilitation, 20,* 1023-1031.